CHAKRAS MASTERY

5 PILLARS TO BALANCE LIFE

CHAKRAS MASTERY

5 PILLARS TO BALANCE LIFE

Authored by

Ajay Pasupulate

WINGS PUBLICATION INTERNATIONAL

WE GIVE WINGS TO YOUR DREAM!

Disclaimer

This book has been published with all reasonable efforts taken to make the material error-free after the consent of the author. This book is sold subject to the condition that it shall not, by way of trade or otherwise, be lent, resold, or otherwise circulated without the copyright owner's prior written consent in any form of binding or cover other than that in which it is published and without a similar condition including this condition being imposed on the subsequent purchaser and without limiting the rights under copyright reserved above, no part of this publication maybe reproduced, stored in or introduced into a retrieval system or transmitted in any form or by any other means without the permission of the copyright owner.

WINGS PUBLICATION INTERNATIONAL
WE GIVE WINGS TO YOUR DREAM!

Registered Office- 907-Sneh Nagar, Sapna Sangeeta Road,
Agrasen Square, Indore – 452001 (M.P.), India
Website: http://www.wingspublication.com
Email: mybook@wingspublication.com

First Published by WINGS PUBLICATION 2024

Title: **CHAKRAS MASTERY: 5 PILLARS TO BALANCE LIFE**
Price: Rs 750 | $29

ISBN 978-93-6006-969-8

LIMITS OF LIABILITY/DISCLAIMER OF WARRANTY

The Author of this book is solely responsible and liable for its content including but not limited to the views, representations, descriptions, statements, information, opinions and references. The information presented in this book is solely compiled by the Author from sources believed to be accurate and the Publisher assumes no responsibility for any errors or omissions. The information is not intended to replace or substitute professional advice.

The Content of this book shall not constitute or be construed or deemed to reflect the opinion or expression of the Publisher. Publisher of this book does not endorse or approve any content of this book or guarantee the reliability, accuracy or completeness of the content published herein and do not make any representations or warranties of any kind, express or implied, including but not limited to the implied warranties of merchantability, fitness for a particular purpose. The Publisher shall not be held liable whatsoever for any errors, omissions, whether such errors or omissions result from negligence, accident, or any other cause or claims for loss or damages of any kind, including without limitation, indirect or consequential loss or damage arising out of use, inability to use, or about the reliability, accuracy or sufficiency of the information contained in this book. All disputes are subject to Indore (M.P.) jurisdiction only.

Special thanks to:

My son **Ketan Pasupulate** (Student)
for proofreading this book.

&

Prakasa Rao for Yoga posture photos

MSc, MPhil, Retired Botany professor

Qualified Yoga practitioner.

Dedication

In humble acknowledgment of the profound impact of the enlightened beings who have graced this world with their presence, this book is dedicated to my Father & Mother, Late Smt. Uma Devi. and the spiritual masters Doctor Newton and Doctor Lakshmi whose teachings go beyond time and space, showing us the way to enlightenment."

Dr Newton and Dr Lakshmi

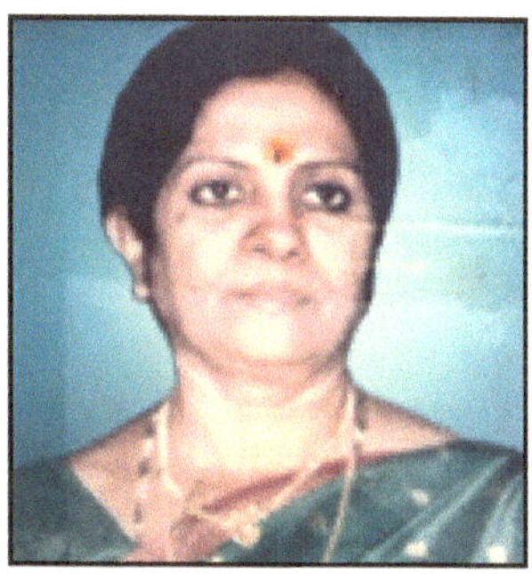

Late Shree Uma Devi

Content

Dedication 1
Acknowledgments 3
Disclaimer 5
Welcome to the Realm of Chakra Mastery 7
Foreword 9
About the book 11

Chapter 1: Root Chakra (Muladhara) 45
Chapter 2: Sacral Chakra (Swadhisthana) 69
Chapter 3: Solar Plexus Chakra (Manipura) 93
Chapter 4: Heart Chakra (Anahata) 117
Chapter 5: Throat Chakra (Vishuddha) 137
Chapter 6: Third Eye Chakra (Ajna) 159
Chapter 7: Crown Chakra (Sahasrara) 193

Revealing The Secrets Of The Akashic Records 215
Lifestyle Vision Chart – Diet And Exercise Plans 223
Magic Plate For Breakfast 227
Gratitude And Giving 231
What Are Your SMART Goals? 235
About Quantum Life University (QLU) 240
PAST LIFE REGRESSION 243
About The Author 248
Testimonials 251
Recommended Books 258

Acknowledgments

My sincere thanks to Shivangi Desai, and other spiritual masters, whose expertise and guidance provided invaluable insights throughout the writing process. Your wisdom and encouragement were instrumental in shaping the content of this book.

Disclaimer

The information provided in this book is for educational and informational purposes only. It is not intended to diagnose, treat, cure, or prevent any disease or medical condition. The techniques and practices described herein are based on traditional wisdom, holistic healing principles, and personal experiences.

Readers are encouraged to consult with qualified healthcare professionals or holistic practitioners before making any changes to their health or wellness routines, especially if they have pre-existing medical conditions or concerns. The author and publisher are not liable for any consequences or outcomes resulting from the use or application of the information presented in this book.

Individual results may vary, and the effectiveness of the techniques and practices described may depend on various factors, including but not limited to individual physiology, health status, and commitment to personal growth and self-care.

By reading this book, you acknowledge and agree to take full responsibility for your health and well-being. You understand that the information provided is not a substitute for professional medical advice, diagnosis, or treatment, and you agree to seek appropriate guidance from qualified healthcare providers as needed.

Welcome to the Realm of *Chakra Mastery*

Dear Reader,

It is with great pleasure that I welcome you to embark on a transformative journey through the pages of 'Chakras Mastery.' Within these sacred teachings, you will discover the profound wisdom of the chakras—the seven energy centres that serve as gateways to our spiritual essence.

Prepare to delve deep into the mysteries of the chakras as we explore their significance, symbolism, and profound impact on our physical, emotional, and spiritual well-being. Through ancient wisdom, modern insights, and practical guidance, you will learn how to awaken, balance, and align your chakras to unleash your full potential and manifest your dreams.

As you navigate this enlightening odyssey, may you open your heart, expand your consciousness, and embrace the infinite possibilities that await you on the path of Chakra Mastery. Trust in the wisdom of your soul, the guidance of the universe, and the transformative power of love.

Welcome, fellow traveller, to the wondrous world of chakras. May this journey bring you profound healing, spiritual awakening, and the realisation of your true divine nature.

With love and light,

Ajay Pasupulate

Foreword

In today's fast-paced world, it's easy to feel disconnected from our inner selves and the powerful energy that is an integral part of who we are. It's essential to recognise that we are not just physical beings but also beings of energy.

The book "Chakras Mastery: 5 Pillars to Balance Life" delves deeply into the concept of chakras, the seven energy centres within our bodies. It provides a comprehensive understanding of how these energy centres impact our physical, mental, emotional, and spiritual well-being in a manner that is accessible and enlightening.

Drawing from ancient wisdom, practical exercises, and insightful guidance, the author, Shri Ajay Pasupulate, who has had profound spiritual experiences, presents a clear and understandable explanation of each chakra. By exploring their attributes and learning how they can bring about personal transformation, readers can gain the knowledge and skills needed to awaken and harmonise their chakras, thus opening themselves up to new opportunities and experiences.

Embarking on the journey of comprehending and balancing our chakras can lead to healing, heightened intuition, increased creativity, and a more profound connection with the world around us. This book serves as a dependable companion, offering the necessary wisdom and techniques to comprehend and engage with our chakras confidently and gracefully, empowering us to unlock our full potential and lead a more harmonious, vibrant, and spiritually enriching life.

I wholeheartedly endorse this book for anyone on a spiritual journey who seeks to tap into the divine energy within us.

Love and Light,

Newton Kondaveti

- Brahmarshi Chakravarti Dr Newton Kondaveti, MBBS, MD is a medical doctor
- Teacher of Meditation and Spiritual Science,
- Pioneer in Past Life Regression, Future Progression and Life Between Lives Regression
- Internationally acclaimed expert on Reincarnation & Law of Karma
- Master teacher of Rebirthing-Breathwork
- Inner Child Work
- Family Constellation and Organizational Constellation work
- Researcher of Paranormal Phenomena
- Expert in Mind Body-Spirit Integration, Energy Medicine, Holistic Healing
- Teacher of Self-Empowerment, Motivational Speaker

About the book

Each chapter delves into the specific characteristics, imbalances, and balancing techniques associated with each chakra, providing readers with a comprehensive understanding and practical tools for chakra balancing.

This book covers all the chakras along with their characteristics, self- tests, and the emotional, physical, and relational impacts of blockages. It also explores the effects of over-energised chakras. Additionally, remedies for balancing chakras such as food, yoga, activities, meditation, and affirmations are discussed.

Why Did I Decide to Write This Book?

I was born and brought up in Hyderabad, India, and migrated to Australia in 2002. At the age of 9, in 1984, a Telugu-language movie on spirituality called 'Sri Madvirat Veerabrahmendra Swamy Charitra' introduced me to chakras. Since then, I searched for a master to teach me the technique. Despite trying various meditation processes over the years, I couldn't connect with any. In 2014, while working as an IT consultant in Canberra, I encountered Shakthi Durga's group of meditators, who practise and teach chakra balancing and healing.

We believe that every person is born with similar abilities and balanced energy centres called chakras. Until the age of 7, everyone has the same natural power and trust. That's why we see young children under 7 as very special. But as we get older, we rely more on thinking logically, which can sometimes imbalance our chakras.

My spiritual journey started when I learned chakra healing and became a practitioner. Things started falling into place for me. I began manifesting things. I wanted a good lifestyle, success in job interviews, business ventures, better health, asset accumulation, building relationships, networking on a large scale, gaining recognition and fame, and financial abundance. In the span of 10 years on my journey, I have manifested everything I desired. Additionally, I have started healing my family and friends whenever necessary. I met Doctor Newton from QLU in Hyderabad, India, who is a spiritual master and joined his group to learn more. I never miss any opportunity to learn from various masters whom I come across.

In December 2023, I attended the Soul Coach program with Dr Newton, where my energy levels increased, and I connected to divine energy. I developed clairvoyance and experienced kundalini awakening, feeling my aura. This inspired me to start reading other people's auras.

Like many others, I used to pray to God or the Universe to fulfil my personal wishes and goals. After achieving most of them, I asked the Universe to guide me in helping people on Earth heal and manifest things in their lives, just as I did in mine. I met Health Coach Guru Shivangi Desai from the 'Fit Bharat Mission' to improve my health, and I am thankful to Spiritual Master Avani Bhadesia, who helped me take my spiritual journey further.

I received the direction to start AJ Life Mastery to reach people in need. I transformed my life, including reversing chronic diseases and other minor health issues, and stopped taking most of my medication.

I designed a transformation program called AJ Life Mastery, focusing on five pillars: Physical, Mental, Emotional, Spiritual, and Financial.

I am grateful to masters like Dr Newton, Shivangi Desai, Swaha Devi, Shakthi Durga, and all other masters who contributed to my transformation.

How to Read This Book?

This book is divided into seven parts for seven chakras.

Firstly, understand what chakras are and where they are located in your body.

Then, do a self-test for each chakra and identify whether it is blocked or not.

Lastly, follow the process of balancing the chakras.

This book helps a person to deal with the outer and inner worlds. So, if you encounter any kind of issue persisting to the physical body or worldly matters at any time, refer to the book and fix it.

How to read this book?

1. Read one chapter per day, clean and activate one chakra per day. Eat food and exercise to balance the chakra.
2. Practise the process for 24 hours.
3. When you move on to the next chakra, then follow it up with the previous chakra process.
4. With every new chakra that you read, you must add the previous chakras for a cumulative effect.
5. By the time you come to the last chapter, you'll already be following the previous chapters.

This might not seem so easy at the beginning. But, believe me, I have practised the chakra balancing for myself and later with my clients. It works like magic. The best part is it's easy. Balancing one chakra a day is not a lot to practise.

This Book is Written on a Single Philosophy

"Tap into the energy centres within; chakra balancing empowers you to manifest your dreams and live your highest truth."

Empower Yourself to Create Your Destiny

How balancing chakras can bring harmony in life for both the present and future generations:

1. Introduction

- *Brief overview of chakras and their significance in Eastern philosophies.*
- *Introduction to the concept of chakra balancing for holistic well-being.*

2. Understanding Chakras

- *Explanation of the seven main chakras and their associated attributes.*

- Discussion on how imbalances in chakras can affect physical, emotional, and spiritual health.

3. Benefits of Chakra Balancing

- *Improved physical health: Discuss how balanced chakras can lead to better overall health and vitality.*
- *Enhanced emotional well-being: Explore how chakra balancing can help manage stress, anxiety, and emotional imbalances.*
- *Heightened spiritual connection: Explain how balanced chakras facilitate a deeper connection to one's higher self and spiritual essence.*

4. Chakra Balancing Techniques

- *Meditation: Guide on using meditation to balance and align chakras, including visualisation techniques and affirmations.*
- *Yoga: Explanation of yoga poses and sequences specifically designed to balance each chakra.*

- *Energy healing: Overview of modalities such as Reiki, acupuncture, and sound therapy for chakra alignment.*

5. Harmony in Present Life

- *Personal testimonials: Real-life stories of individuals who have experienced positive transformations through chakra balancing.*
- *Case studies: Examples of how chakra balancing has improved relationships, career success, and overall well-being.*

6. Legacy for Future Generations

- *Importance of holistic health: Discuss how balanced chakras contribute to a healthier, happier life for individuals and their families.*
- *Cultivating mindfulness: Discover how doing chakra balancing helps kids and adults to be more aware of themselves and stay focused.*
- *Passing down traditions: Encouragement to teach children and grandchildren about chakras and holistic wellness practices.*

7. Conclusion

- *Recap of the benefits of chakra balancing for present and future generations.*
- *Call to action for readers to prioritise chakra balancing as a means to create harmony and well-being for themselves and future generations.*

This content outline provides a structured approach to discussing how balancing chakras can bring harmony in life not only for the present but also for future generations, emphasising the importance of holistic health and mindfulness practices.

Note: Balancing all the chakras at once might be difficult for most people because we're often dealing with everyday life.

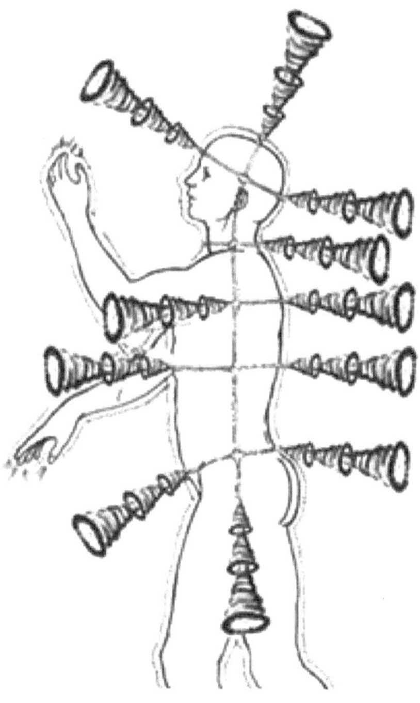

Guided meditations and workshops are available in the AJ Life Mastery portal. www.ajlifemastery.com

Background:

The naming of chakras originates from ancient Indian

spiritual and philosophical traditions, particularly within the context of yoga, tantra, and Ayurveda. The word "chakra" itself is derived from Sanskrit, an ancient Indo-Aryan language, and it translates to "wheel" or "circle" in English. Chinese call these energy centres as Meridians which are used in acupuncture. Meridians and chakras are related concepts but are distinct in terms of their functions and characteristics.

Meridians are channels in the body through which vital energy, known as "qi" or "chi" in traditional Chinese medicine, flows. There are twelve main meridians in the body, each associated with specific organs and functions. The flow of energy through these meridians is believed to be essential for maintaining health and well-being in traditional Chinese medicine.

Chakras, on the other hand, are energy centres located along the central channel of the body, from the base of the spine to the crown of the head, according to Hindu and Buddhist traditions. There are typically seven main chakras, each associated with different aspects of physical, emotional, and spiritual well-being.

While both meridians and chakras are believed to be involved in the flow and regulation of energy in the body, they have different origins, systems of understanding, and functions. Meridians are more closely associated with traditional Chinese medicine, while chakras are integral to Hindu and Buddhist spiritual practices.

It is understood that there are over 141 energy centres,

known as chakras, in the human body. Among these are the Alpha and Omega chakras, with the Alpha chakra, often called the Father, positioned atop the head above the Sahasrara chakra. Conversely, the Omega chakra, referred to as the Mother, is located in the feet, symbolising grounding to Mother Earth.

The concept of chakras can be found in various ancient texts, including the Vedas, Upanishads, and Tantras. These texts describe subtle energy centres within the human body, which are believed to play a significant role in physical, emotional, and spiritual well-being.

The specific names assigned to each chakra are often associated with their location within the body and their corresponding qualities and functions. For example:

1. The Root Chakra (Muladhara) is located at the base of the spine, with "mula" meaning "root" and "adhara" meaning "support." It is associated with survival, stability, and grounding.
2. The Sacral Chakra (Swadhisthana) is located in the lower abdomen, with "swa" meaning "one's own" and "sthana" meaning "dwelling place." It is associated with creativity, pleasure, and emotions.
3. The Solar Plexus Chakra (Manipura) is located in the upper abdomen, with "manipura" meaning "city of jewels." It is associated with personal power, self-esteem, and transformation.
4. The Heart Chakra (Anahata) is located in the centre

of the chest, with "anahata" meaning "unstruck" or "unhurt." It is associated with love, compassion, and connection.

5. The Throat Chakra (Vishuddha) is located in the throat region, with "vishuddha" meaning "purification." It is associated with communication, self-expression, and truth.
6. The Third Eye Chakra (Ajna) is located in the forehead, between the eyebrows, with "ajna" meaning "command" and "perceive." It is associated with intuition, insight, and spiritual awareness.
7. The Crown Chakra (Sahasrara) is located at the top of the head, with "sahasrara" meaning "thousand-petalled." It is associated with divine consciousness, spiritual connection, and enlightenment.

Overall, the naming of chakras reflects their significance and symbolism within the spiritual and energetic framework of the human body, as described in ancient Indian texts and traditions.

While these seven chakras are the most widely recognised, some traditions may acknowledge additional chakras or energy centres within the body. However, the focus of most teachings and practices revolves around these primary seven chakras.

The human body is the vessel for the soul's earthly experience.

The human body becomes the vehicle through which the soul experiences life on Earth. The soul, like a driver, uses the human body as a car to travel through life. Just as we drive cars to go places, the soul uses our bodies to experience life on Earth. It's like wearing a special suit that lets us feel and do things. Through our bodies, the soul learns and grows, feeling happy, sad, and everything in between. Every action we take, and every feeling we have is like a journey for the soul. Together, our bodies and souls make a team, exploring the world and making memories along the way.

For a smooth journey, the body needs to be maintained to experience life on Earth. In this modern world, people have no time to look after their bodies and lack direction. They suffer from health issues, poverty, crises, and political disturbances globally. Since the recent pandemic, there has been a shift in energy on Earth, leading to changes and a new normal. Online transactions, working from home, new startups, and old businesses shutting down have become common occurrences. Middle-aged housewives are starting new careers, and some employers have become employees while employees have become employers. In this fast-paced and unpredictable life, humans need direction to survive, meet their needs, maintain relationships, and cope with insecurity, anxiety, depression, and diseases. Thanks to our ancestors who discovered the human manual called chakras to help navigate day-to-day life.

Human Manual:

When you purchase any product, such as electronic goods, a vehicle, or even a toy, it typically includes a manual. This manual provides instructions on how to set up and operate the product. For instance, a car comes with a manual that remains with it until it is scrapped. Similarly, human beings also have a manual called chakras. One should understand how to 'drive' this vehicle, i.e., the body. If any issues arise during the lifespan, one should be capable of addressing those problems, whether they involve the inner or outer world. Just as a car requires fuel, regular servicing, and cleaning, our human body also requires energy to function along with regular cleaning and maintenance.

PS: The inner body refers to the physical body, and the outer body refers to activities in the outside world.

Welcome to the beginning of our journey

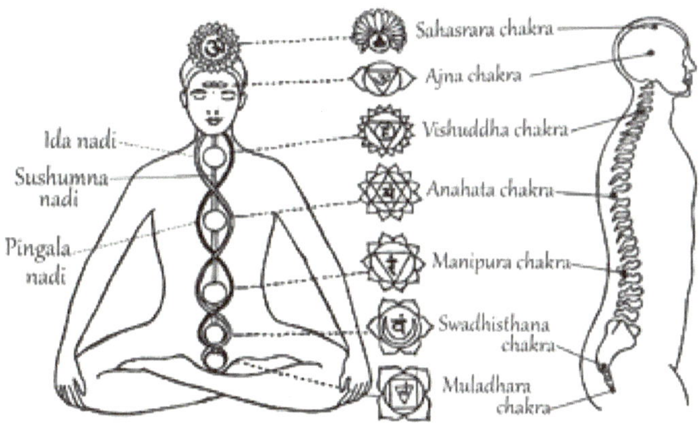

Relative positions of Chakras in Pranamaya kosa

Chakras in Conjunction with Meditation:

Chakras play a vital role in meditation, serving as focal points for channelling energy and promoting inner balance. By aligning and activating the chakras during meditation, practitioners can enhance.

When humans are born, they have ESP, trust in others, and trust in the universe. For example, when an adult plays with a toddler, tossing them into the air and catching them, the toddler laughs even though it may seem scary because they trust the adult. However, that same adult may not trust others in similar situations.

Through meditation, I got ESP, where I developed intuitive abilities.

Every human on the earth has the ability to develop psychic or intuitive abilities. Due to the worldly matters dealing with day-to-day life humans are exposed to negative energies.

In various spiritual and alternative medicine traditions, negative energies that are believed to block human abilities, such as ESP (extrasensory perception), are often associated with concepts like psychic or energetic blockages. These blockages are thought to hinder the flow of energy throughout the body, affecting one's ability to access and develop psychic or intuitive abilities.

Some common sources or causes of negative energies and blockages may include:

1. Emotional trauma: Past or present emotional wounds, unresolved conflicts, or traumatic experiences can

create energetic blockages that affect mental and emotional well-being.

2. Stress and negative emotions: Chronic stress, anxiety, fear, anger, or other negative emotions can disrupt the flow of energy in the body and interfere with clarity of perception and intuition.
3. Environmental factors: Unhealthy or energetically imbalanced environments, exposure to electromagnetic radiation, and negative influences from other people or places can contribute to energetic disturbances.
4. Unhealthy lifestyle habits: Poor diet, lack of exercise, substance abuse, and other unhealthy lifestyle habits can affect overall energy levels and vitality, potentially leading to blockages in the energetic system.
5. Limited belief systems: Negative beliefs, self-doubt, and limiting beliefs about one's own abilities can create psychological barriers that hinder the development and expression of psychic or intuitive gifts.

Practices such as meditation, energy healing, chakra balancing, aura cleansing, and spiritual practices are often employed to address these blockages and promote energetic balance and well-being. Additionally, seeking support from trained practitioners or therapists who specialise in energy work or holistic healing modalities can be helpful in identifying and addressing negative energies and blockages.

Through focused attention and visualisation techniques,

individuals can clear blockages within the chakras, allowing for a smoother flow of energy throughout the body. This harmonious energy flow fosters deep relaxation, heightened awareness, and a profound sense of inner peace. Incorporating chakra meditation into one's practice can lead to greater clarity of mind, heightened intuition, and a deeper connection to the self and the universe.

There are several ways to meditate. A simple technique involves observing your breath flowing in and out. Thoughts will arise; simply observe them as they come and go, similar to watching stations pass by when travelling by train. One can meditate according to one's age; for instance, if you're 35 years old, meditate for 35 minutes.

Ten-step process on chakra meditation.

1. Sit comfortably, either on the floor or in a chair, with a straight back.
2. Close your eyes and breathe normally, observing the inflow and outflow of your breath.
3. Imagine a white pillar of light flowing from the universe, passing through your head, neck, upper body, and lower body. Visualise yourself being filled with white light energy.
4. Ground yourself by imagining your Root Chakra, or the tailbone spine's L5, growing like the roots of a tree into the centre of the earth, anchoring you firmly.
5. Visualise a red-coloured wheel spinning from your Root Chakra, clearing any black spots or blockages and filling

the area with red light.

6. Repeat this process for each chakra, visualising spinning wheels clearing blockages.
7. Finally, visualise the Crown Chakra opening like lotus petals on your head, allowing the Aum symbol to penetrate.
8. Maintain this state for as long as possible, focusing on the chakras rotating and filling you with bright light while your entire body is engulfed in white, violet, or indigo light.
9. Before concluding, feel an energy ball between your palms, as if pressing a balloon. Once you sense the energy ball with your chosen colour, place it over your head and cover your entire body.
10. When ready, rub your palms together, place them over your eyes, and slowly open your eyes.

Practise this chakra meditation daily to balance your chakras amidst exposure to the external world.

Note: It may not always be possible for all chakras to be balanced simultaneously for the average individual.

Chakras and their Alignments in Conjunction with the Aura, Ida, Pingala, and Sushumna Energy Pathways:

The aura, often described as the subtle energy field surrounding the human body, is intricately connected with the chakras, Ida, Pingala, and Sushumna energy pathways. Each layer of the aura corresponds to different aspects of the physical, emotional, mental, and spiritual self, and these layers interact with the chakras and energy pathways to maintain overall balance and well-being. They are 1/10th the size of human hair.

The chakras serve as focal points within the aura, regulating the flow of energy throughout the subtle body. When the chakras are balanced and aligned, they emit vibrant energy that harmonises and strengthens the aura, promoting vitality and health. Conversely, imbalances or blockages in the chakras can disrupt the flow of energy within the

aura, leading to various physical, emotional, or spiritual disturbances.

The Ida and Pingala energy pathways, often depicted as spiralling channels of energy, intersect with the chakras and influence the flow of prana or life force energy throughout the body. The Sushumna energy pathway, running along the spine, serves as the central channel for spiritual energy, connecting the individual with higher states of consciousness.

By working with practices such as meditation, yoga, and energy healing, individuals can harmonise and balance the chakras and energy pathways, thereby restoring equilibrium to the aura and promoting overall well-being on all levels of existence.

Ayurveda and its Alignments in Conjunction with the Chakras, Aura, Ida, Pingala, and Sushumna Energy Pathways:

Ayurveda, the ancient Indian system of medicine, recognises the intimate connection between the physical body, mind, and spirit, and its principles align closely with the concepts of the aura, chakras, and energy pathways such as Ida, Pingala, and Sushumna. In Ayurveda, the body is viewed as a microcosm of the universe, and health is achieved through balance and harmony within the body's energies.

Ayurveda acknowledges the existence of subtle energy channels, or nadis, which correspond to the Ida and Pingala pathways described in yogic traditions. These nadis intersect with the chakras, which are considered vital energy centres within the body. When the chakras are balanced and the nadis are free-flowing, optimal health and well-being are achieved.

The aura, according to Ayurveda, reflects an individual's overall state of health and vitality. A balanced aura indicates good physical, mental, and emotional health, while disturbances in the aura may signal underlying imbalances or blockages in the chakras and energy pathways.

Ayurvedic practices such as yoga, meditation, herbal remedies, and lifestyle adjustments aim to restore balance to the body's energies, thereby promoting healing and wellness on all levels. By aligning with the principles of

Ayurveda, individuals can enhance their overall vitality and cultivate a deeper connection with their inner selves and the world around them.

In Ayurveda, the human body is classified into different types or categories based on various factors such as constitution, doshas (bio-energies), and the state of balance or imbalance. Here are the main types of bodies recognised in Ayurveda:

1. **Prakriti (Constitutional Body Type):** Prakriti refers to an individual's unique constitution, determined at birth by the predominance of the three doshas: Vata, Pitta, and Kapha. Each person has a unique combination of these doshas, which influences their physical, mental, and emotional characteristics.

2. **Sharira (Physical Body):** Sharira refers to the physical body, including the organs, tissues, and systems. Ayurveda recognises the importance of maintaining the balance and health of the physical body through proper diet, lifestyle, and therapeutic interventions.

3. **Sthula Sharira (Gross Physical Body):** Sthula Sharira refers to the gross or tangible aspect of the physical body, including the organs, muscles, bones, and skin. It is the physical manifestation of the subtle energies within the body.

4. **Sukshma Sharira (Subtle Body):** Sukshma Sharira refers to the subtle or energetic aspect of the body, including the nadis (energy channels), chakras (energy centres), and prana (life force energy). It is the energetic

template that influences the physical body and reflects the individual's spiritual essence.

5. **Karana Sharira (Causal Body):** Karana Sharira refers to the causal or the karmic aspect of the body, which is beyond the physical and subtle realms. It is the repository of past karmas (actions) and influences the individual's destiny and spiritual evolution.

Understanding and balancing these different aspects of the body is essential for promoting health, harmony, and overall well-being according to the Ayurvedic principles.

Energy Points at Kasi/ Varanasi:

I would like to share my experience visiting the energy points in the city of Kasi, India, known as the Sun Points, which are high-energy locations.

Chakras are wheels of energy in the world. It is a known fact that the Universe, our human body, and other living beings and objects are made of energy. In our human body, the nadis Ida and Pingala, when they intersect, form a circle and create energy centres. These energy centres are called chakras, which determine human beings' inner (physical body) and outer (external world) lifestyle.

In the city of Kasi (also known as Varanasi) in India, there are 12 significant points associated with the sun's energy. These points are often referred to as the "Dwadash Aditya" (Twelve Suns) and are considered sacred in Hindu mythology and spirituality. They are believed to represent different manifestations or aspects of the sun god, Surya. These points include temples, ghats (riverfront steps), and sacred sites along the banks of the Ganges River, each with its own significance and mythological stories associated with it. Some of the notable points include the Adi Keshava Temple, Adi Varaha Temple, and the Assi Ghat, among others. These sites are visited by pilgrims and devotees seeking spiritual blessings and enlightenment.

In 2018, I visited the city of Varanasi in India, where I explored eight energy points out of several Sun Points that activate chakras. They are found at various locations on the banks of the river Ganga, known as ghats. It is believed in some cultures, especially in the Hindu religion, that visiting sacred places and staying there for a while can fulfil our wishes. For example, couples facing infertility issues may be advised to visit specific temples and perform prayers. Most of these sacred places have high energy levels that activate the Sacral Chakra.

Many health and external world issues were resolved when people visited such sacred places. We see millions of people visiting these pilgrimage sites to fulfil their wishes, including saints called Naga Sadhus and Aghoras, who have mastered chakras.

After visiting the Sun Points, my chakras were highly energised, and it took me almost four weeks to balance them.

Below are some of the Sun Points associated with chakras.

1. Uttarark Aditya - poverty - UV radiation
2. Keshav Aditya - sin
3. Sumantva Aditya - leprosy
4. Khakholkh Aditya - sin
5. Arun Aditya - sorrow
6. Mayukh Aditya - poverty
7. Samba Aditya – leprosy, skin disease
8. Yama Aditya - fear of death

9. Ganga Aditya - water-sun duality
10. Draupad Aditya - hunger
11. Vriddh Aditya - suffering from old age
12. Vimal Aditya - leprosy
13. Karna Aditya
14. Lolark Aditya - infertility

I have had many personal experiences after learning chakra healing. My first experience of healing others occurred in 2015 when a friend experienced a trauma and collapsed. After assessing the person, I was able to heal them. Subsequently, this individual discovered the power of chakra balancing and has since become a renowned spiritual master.

This incident boosted my confidence in my ability to transform people's lives by balancing their chakras. Since then, I have helped many individuals in need. Now, I am a full-time spiritual master and have launched Aj Life Mastery to reach a global audience.

Another energy place is the Quantum Life University campus. I attended the Soul Coach Program (SCP) in December 2023 for 10 days. It was an amazing spiritual journey where I learned from various masters. The 6th and 7th days of the program were focussed on Chakras, Kundalini, and Aura. I felt my chakras activated, experienced Kundalini awakening, and found myself able to read other people's aura. I began to "see" things beyond the physical realm, receiving visual images, symbols, or impressions about past, present, and future events. Additionally, I was able to hear Mahatma Patri Ji's clairaudience (hearing that which is inaudible) and learned valuable lessons about not judging masters.

The region itself possesses so much energy that it transformed my life to the next level. I am not typically a book reader, and I hardly have a collection of books at home, most of which I have never read. However, after the SCP, I started reading books and am now even writing them. Apart from this, I have seen my business pick up, experienced a better financial flow, built a network, improved my bank balance, gained recognition, and acquired new learnings. I see every minor

wish of mine come true. I would like to share one small wish of mine with you about how it manifested. I always had a wish to buy a good quality Rudraksha bead necklace but was unsure which one to wear and where to find good quality beads. During the SCP, I met a master who wore beads, and I wished I could get one for myself as well. To my surprise, within 10 days, I happened to make an unplanned trip to Srisailam on a pilgrimage and came across Rudraksha bead necklaces with up to 14 faces (Mukhas). I bought one, offered it to Lord Shiva, and wore it. The following week, I visited Somnath and received blessings from Lord Shiva. I am thankful to Dr Newton, who gave me the opportunity to transform my life and manifest things.

Chakras in Summary

The following tables provide a summary of the chakras along with their associations with colour, sound, energy points, and affirmations.

Chakras	Sanskrit Name	Element	Colour	Sound / Mantra	Energy
Root	Muladhara	Earth	Red	Lam	Survival and Grounding
Sacral	Swadostana	Water	Orange	Vam	Emotions, Feelings, Desire
Solar Plexus Heart	Manipura Anahaat	Fire Air	Yellow Green	Ram Yam	Pleasure, Sexuality Will, Power, Love & Relationship
Throat	Vishuddha	Sound sky	Blue	Ham	Communication, Creativity
Third Eye Crown	Agna Sahasrara	Light Thought	Indigo Violet or White	OM OM	Intuitive, Clarity, Vision Wisdom, Awareness, Intelligence

Chakras	Candle Colour	Fragrance	Crystals
Root	Red	Spikenard	Garnet (Red)
Sacral	Orange	Lemon Flavour	Rose Quartz (light pink)
Solar Plexus	Yellow	Jasmine	Yellow Jade or Citrine
Heart	Green	Rose	Green Aventurine
Throat	Blue	Lavender	Clear Quartz(looks like broken)
Third Eye	Indigo	Sandalwood	Sodalite (Indigo blue, light)
Crown	Violet	Frankincense	Amethyst (Purple/violet)

Daily Affirmations to shift the energy.

Root Chakra	I am safe and protected. I love my life I am rich and grounded
Sacral Chakra	I allow my creativity to flow through me freely I am comfortable in my body, and I treat it with care. I enjoy pleasure in all areas of my life.
Solar Plexus Chakra	I am worthy I am confident in all that I do
Heart Chakra	I can easily let go of my past. I forgive myself and others I love myself, and I am loved by others
Throat Chakra	I speak my truth confidently I express my wisdom comfortably I am a very good listener
Third Eye Chakra	I seek to understand and learn from my life experience I am able to see and act in alignment with my divine purpose My intuition is highly accurate and clear
Crown Chakra	I am receptive to divine messages I am divinely inspired and guided by the universe. I am a spiritual being in the human body

Benefits of Chakra Balancing

Improved physical health: Discuss how balanced chakras can lead to better overall health and vitality. Enhanced emotional well-being: Explore how chakra balancing can help manage stress, anxiety, and emotional imbalances.

SPIRITUALITY

Chakras balancing - self assessment

Heightened spiritual connection:

Explain how balanced chakras facilitate a deeper connection to one's higher self and spiritual essence.

Answer each of the question to know your chakra is balanced or not?

N = NEVER	P = POOR	N OR P is 1
S = SELDOM	F = FAIR	S OR F is 2
O = OFTEN	G =GOOD	O OR G is 3
A = ALWAYS	E= EXCELLENT	A OR E is 4

1.Root chakra - Earth, survival, Grounding

Questions	Answer	Score
How often you go to woods or spend time in nature	N S O A	
How often do you exercise (Yoga, Gym, Body weightsetc)	N S O A	
How is your relationship with money and work?	P F G E	
How is your rate your physical health	P F G E	
Do you feel secured?	N S O A	
Do you love your body?	N S O A	
Do you feel you have a right to live in this world	N S O A	
	Total	

2.Sacral chakra- Water, Emotions, Sexuality

Questions	Answer	Score
How would you rate your ability to fee and express emotions?	P F G E	
How is your sex life?	P F G E	
Do you take much time create simple pleasure in your life	N S O A	
How would you rate you physical ability?	P F G E	
How would you rate your emotional ability?	P F G E	
Are you able to nurture or be nurtured by other in balance	N S O A	
Do you struggle with guilt about your feelings or sexuality?	A O S N	
	Total	

3. Solar Plexus chakra- Fire , Power, Will

Questions	Answer	Score
How would you rate your general energy level?	P F G E	
How would you rate your metabolism / obesity.	P F G E	
Do you feel a lack of drive, determination, and direction in life?	N S O A	
Are you always trying to fit in and please others?	A O S N	
Are you always seeking confirmation from others?	A O S N	
Do you often fee tiredness and fatigue?	A O S N	
Do you feel guilty and ashamed when you say "no" to people	N S O A	
	Total	

4. Heart chakra- Air, Love, Relationship

Questions	Answer	Score
Do you love yourself?	N S O A	
Do you have successful long-term relationships?	N S O A	
Are you to accept the people they way they are?	N S O A	
Do you share? Food, things, advice,knowledge, results in growth and fulfilment.	N S O A	
Do you carry lot of grief in your heart?	A O S N	
How is your breathing, it is normal, shallow or deep?	P F G E	
Do you forgive others?May not straight away but later?	N S O A	
	Total	

5.Throat chakra- Sound, Communication, Creativity

Questions	Answer	Score
Are you a good listener?	N S O A	
Do you like to write your thoughts and feeling, whether on social media or elsewhere?	N S O A	
Are you organized? Creative in organizing?	N S O A	
Do you engage in any kind of art form(painting, singing etc)	N S O A	
Are you good at convincing others?	P F G E	
Do you feel "in sync" with life?	N S O A	
Are you good at communication?	N S O A	
	Total	

6.Third eye chakra- Light, Intuition, Seeing

Questions	Answer	Score
How would you rate your ability to visualize?	P F G E	
Do you listen to your inner voice?	N S O A	
Do you enjoy learning new things?	N S O A	
Do you believe in universal energy?	N S O A	
Do you have vivid dreams (and remember them)	N S O A	
Are you a keen observer?	N S O A	
Do you notice subtle visual details in your surroundings?	N S O A	
	Total	

7.Crown chakra- Thoughts, Awareness, Wisdom, Intelligence

Questions	Answer	Score
Do you meditate?	N S O A	
Are you open new ideas?	N S O A	
Are you aware of illusion and reality? For example, closing your eyes during the day time	N S O A	
Do you feel strong connection with some kind of higher energy or power or God, spirit etc.	N S O A	
Are you able to release doubt and welcome faith?	N S O A	
Do you mostly live in the present in your thoughts?	N S O A	
	Total	

- Add score for each chakra and compare

Score of each chakra

28-22 = very strong chakra

13-21 = average - need improvement

6-12 = weak chakra - Need to work on chakra(s)

Clients – Results to be displayed with below notes.

Compare the highest and lowest chakra scores and evaluate whether this pattern aligns with your own perceptions of yourself. This analysis will help you understand if the chakra assessment resonates with your self-view and can provide insights into areas of balance or imbalance within your energy system.

CHAPTER 1

ROOT CHAKRA (MULADHARA)

The Root Chakra, or Muladhara, is the foundational energy centre located at the base of the spine. Represented by the colour red, it symbolises stability, security, and our connection to the physical world. This chakra governs our basic survival needs, including food, shelter, and safety. When the Root Chakra is balanced, we feel grounded, secure, and rooted in our existence.

However, imbalances in the Root Chakra can manifest as feelings of insecurity, fear, and instability. Physical symptoms may include issues with the lower back, legs, or feet. Emotional and mental imbalances might lead to anxiety, financial concerns, or a sense of disconnection from the world around us.

To restore balance to the Root Chakra, various techniques can be employed. These may include grounding meditation practices, yoga poses that focus on the lower body, and affirmations that reinforce feelings of safety and stability. Additionally, activities that connect us with nature, such as walking barefoot on the earth or gardening, can help to strengthen the Root Chakra.

By nurturing and balancing the Root Chakra, we can

cultivate a solid foundation upon which to build our lives, enabling us to feel more secure, grounded, and empowered in our journey towards holistic well-being.

The Root Chakra, or Muladhara in Sanskrit, is the first of the seven main chakras located at the base of the spine. It serves as the foundation of the chakra system, representing our connection to the physical world, survival instincts, and sense of security.

Location - positioned at the base of the spine, near the coccyx or tailbone. It is the first of the seven main chakras in the body, located at the perineum, which is the area between the genitals and the anus.

- Element - Earth
- Colour – Red
- Sound - Lam
- Energy – Life force
- Gland – Adrenal
- Crystal - Red Jasper, Smoky Quartz, Bloodstone
- Aroma - Cedarwood, Vetiver, Frankincense, Myrrh, Ginger, Sandalwood, Spikenard,
- Produce a variety of hormones such as adrenaline, steroids, aldosterone and cortisol.
- Their functions include the regulation of metabolism and the Immune system.
- Sense – Smell
- Deals with survival, grounding, security and stability

Characteristics of the Root Chakra:

1. Stability and Security - The Root Chakra governs our basic survival needs, including food, shelter, and safety. When balanced, it provides a sense of stability, security, and rootedness in our existence.
2. Grounding - This chakra anchors us to the earth, fostering a sense of grounding and connection to the physical world. It helps us feel present, centred, and in tune with our surroundings.
3. Physical Health - The Root Chakra influences the health of the physical body, particularly the lower back, legs, and feet. It supports overall vitality and well-being.
4. Trust and Safety - A balanced Root Chakra fosters feelings of trust in oneself and the world, as well as a sense of safety and security in one's environment and relationships.
5. Survival Instincts - This chakra governs our primal instincts for survival, including the fight-or-flight response, ensuring our basic needs are met for survival.
6. Manifestation - The Root Chakra is associated with manifestation and materialisation, supporting our ability to bring our desires and goals into physical reality.

Overall, the Root Chakra serves as the foundation for our spiritual journey, providing the stability and security necessary for growth, transformation, and self-realisation.

Balancing and nurturing this chakra is essential for overall well-being and a sense of groundedness in life.

Self-Test:

Answer in Yes or No

1. Are you comfortable with your physical body?
2. Do you rarely get sick?
3. Are you self-inspired?
4. Do you achieve most of your goals?
5. Are you very passionate about most things?
6. Are you willing to fight for justice?
7. Do you have a strong drive to live?
8. Do you feel that you have a right to exist?
9. Are you able to put your thoughts into action? Are you over-thinking?
10. Is money and home very important to you?

Results:

Check if your answer is Yes or No. If you get Yes, then see the results below;

8-10 – Excellent

5-7 – Good

2-4 – can be better

0-1 – Best of luck

If Blocked:

The Root Chakra can become blocked or imbalanced due to various factors related to physical, emotional, and mental well-being. Here are some common situations or circumstances that may contribute to a blocked Root Chakra:

1. Trauma or Childhood Wounds - Early experiences of neglect, abandonment, or instability can create deep-rooted feelings of insecurity and fear, leading to blockages in the Root Chakra.
2. Financial Stress - Issues related to money, such as financial instability, debt, or unemployment, can trigger feelings of insecurity and anxiety, contributing to Root Chakra imbalances.
3. Disconnection from Nature - Living in urban environments or spending little time in nature can disrupt our connection to the earth, leading to feelings of disconnection and ungroundedness.
4. Physical Illness or Injury - Chronic physical ailments, injuries, or conditions affecting the lower body, such as lower back pain or hip problems, can impact the Root Chakra's energy flow.
5. Lack of Safety or Stability - Experiencing environments or relationships characterised by instability, conflict, or abuse can create a sense of insecurity and mistrust, leading to blockages in the Root Chakra.
6. Unresolved Fear or Anxiety - Persistent feelings of

fear, anxiety, or worry about survival needs, such as food, shelter, or personal safety, can disrupt the Root Chakra's energy flow.

7. Unhealthy Lifestyle Habits - Poor diet, lack of exercise, substance abuse, or excessive consumption of material goods can contribute to Root Chakra imbalances by reinforcing feelings of instability and disconnection.
8. Stressful Life Events - Major life changes, such as moving to a new city, loss of a loved one, or relationship difficulties, can disrupt the Root Chakra's energy flow and trigger feelings of insecurity and instability.
9. Cultural or Familial Beliefs - Cultural or familial beliefs that undermine one's sense of security or self-worth can contribute to Root Chakra imbalances by fostering feelings of inadequacy or unworthiness.
10. Spiritual Disconnection - Lack of spiritual connection or purpose can lead to feelings of emptiness or lack of grounding, contributing to Root Chakra blockages.

Emotional Impacts:

Emotionally and mentally, a blocked Root Chakra can result in deep-seated fears, insecurities, and a pervasive sense of anxiety. You may constantly worry about your basic survival needs being met, such as food, shelter, and financial security. This fear-based mentality can lead to feelings of unworthiness, powerlessness, and an inability to trust yourself or others.

1. Fear and Anxiety - A blocked Root Chakra can lead to heightened feelings of fear and anxiety, particularly related to survival needs such as food, shelter, and safety. Individuals may experience irrational fears, constant worry, or a sense of impending danger.
2. Insecurity - Feelings of insecurity and instability are common when the Root Chakra is blocked. Individuals may lack confidence in themselves or their abilities and may constantly seek external validation or reassurance.
3. Low Self-Esteem - A blocked Root Chakra can contribute to feelings of inadequacy or unworthiness. Individuals may struggle with self-doubt, negative self-talk, and a persistent sense of not being good enough.
4. Trust Issues - Difficulty in trusting oneself or others is another common emotional issue associated with a blocked Root Chakra. Individuals may have a fear of betrayal or abandonment and may struggle to form healthy, trusting relationships.
5. Feeling Disconnected - A blocked Root Chakra can create a sense of disconnection from oneself, others, and the world around them. Individuals may feel emotionally numb, disconnected from their bodies, or unable to fully engage with life.
6. Depression - Feelings of depression and hopelessness can arise when the Root Chakra is blocked. Individuals may experience a lack of motivation, energy, and enthusiasm for life, as well as feelings of emptiness or

despair.

7. Mood Swings - Emotional instability and mood swings may occur when the Root Chakra is blocked. Individuals may experience sudden shifts in mood, from anger and irritability to sadness and despair, without clear triggers.
8. Resistance to Change - A blocked Root Chakra can create resistance to change and a fear of stepping out of one's comfort zone. Individuals may cling to familiar routines, habits, or beliefs, even if they are no longer serving them.
9. Materialism and Greed - Excessive focus on material possessions and wealth can be a manifestation of a blocked Root Chakra. Individuals may seek external sources of security and validation through material wealth, leading to feelings of greed or possessiveness.
10. Lack of Purpose - A blocked Root Chakra can contribute to feelings of aimlessness or lack of direction in life. Individuals may struggle to find meaning or purpose, feeling disconnected from their true desires and passions.

These emotional and mental issues can significantly impact one's overall well-being and quality of life. By addressing the root causes of Root Chakra blockages and implementing holistic healing practices, individuals can work towards restoring balance and promoting a greater sense of security, stability, and groundedness in their lives.

Relationship Impacts:

The Root Chakra, associated with our sense of security, stability, and foundation, can significantly impact our relationships. Here are the top five relationship impacts associated with the Root Chakra:

1. Trust Issues - A balanced Root Chakra fosters feelings of security and trust in relationships. However, imbalances in this chakra, such as feelings of insecurity or instability, can lead to trust issues in relationships. This may manifest as difficulty trusting others, fear of betrayal, or an inability to rely on partners.
2. Co-dependency - When the Root Chakra is imbalanced, individuals may seek external sources of security and validation to compensate for inner feelings of insecurity. This can result in codependent relationships, where individuals rely excessively on their partners for emotional support, validation, or a sense of identity.
3. Fear of Abandonment - The Root Chakra is closely tied to our sense of safety and belonging. Imbalances in this chakra, such as unresolved childhood traumas or experiences of abandonment, can lead to a fear of abandonment in adult relationships. Individuals may exhibit clingy behaviour, fear of being alone, or difficulty forming secure attachments.
4. Conflict and Power Struggles - Imbalances in the Root Chakra can manifest as power struggles or conflicts within relationships. When individuals feel insecure or threatened, they may resort to controlling behaviour,

manipulation, or dominance to maintain a sense of control or security in the relationship.

5. Difficulty Establishing Boundaries - A balanced Root Chakra supports the ability to establish healthy boundaries in relationships, respecting one's own needs and the needs of others. However, imbalances in this chakra can lead to difficulties in setting and maintaining boundaries. Individuals may struggle to assert themselves, tolerate mistreatment, or have difficulty saying no to others.

Addressing Root Chakra imbalances through practices such as grounding exercises, inner child healing, and self-care can help improve relationship dynamics and promote greater security, stability, and trust in interpersonal connections. Therapy, couples counselling, and communication skills training can also provide valuable support in navigating relationship challenges associated with Root Chakra imbalances.

Physical Impacts:

The Root Chakra, also known as the Muladhara Chakra, is associated with the physical body's foundation, stability, and sense of security. Imbalances or blockages in the Root Chakra can manifest in various physical symptoms. Here are the top five physical impacts associated with the Root Chakra:

1. Digestive Issues - The Root Chakra governs the digestive system and elimination processes. Imbalances in this chakra may lead to digestive problems such as constipation, diarrhoea, irritable bowel syndrome (IBS), or other gastrointestinal issues.
2. Lower Back Pain - The Root Chakra is located at the base of the spine, so imbalances can manifest as lower back pain, stiffness, or discomfort. Chronic lower back pain may indicate unresolved issues related to security, stability, or feeling grounded.
3. Fatigue and Weakness - A blocked or imbalanced Root Chakra can result in feelings of fatigue, lethargy, or lack of physical energy. This may manifest as chronic tiredness, weakness, or a general lack of vitality.
4. Immune System Disorders - The Root Chakra is associated with the body's ability to defend itself against illness and maintain overall health. Imbalances in this chakra may weaken the immune system, making individuals more susceptible to infections, allergies, or autoimmune disorders.
5. Foot and Leg Problems - As the Root Chakra is connected to the feet and legs, imbalances can manifest as issues in these areas. This may include foot pain, leg cramps, gout, circulation problems, or issues with mobility and balance.

Addressing imbalances in the Root Chakra through practices such as meditation, yoga, grounding exercises, and energy healing can help alleviate these physical symptoms and promote overall well-being. Additionally, seeking guidance from healthcare professionals can provide support in managing and treating any underlying physical conditions.

Overall, a blocked Root Chakra can leave you feeling profoundly ungrounded, fearful, and disconnected from yourself and the world around you. Healing practices that focus on grounding, stability, and self-care can help to release blockages and restore balance to the Root Chakra, enabling you to feel more secure, grounded, and empowered in your life.

If Over Energised:

When the Root Chakra is over-energised, it can lead to an imbalance characterised by excessive attachment to material possessions, overindulgence, and a lack of grounding. This excess energy in the Root Chakra can manifest physically, emotionally, and mentally. Emotional and mental symptoms include being:

- Angry
- Greedy
- Aggressive
- Unfriendly
- Materialistic
- Double-faced
- Power-hungry

Physically, an over-energised Root Chakra may result in hyperactivity, restlessness, and an inability to relax. You might experience sensations of jitteriness, insomnia, or digestive issues due to excessive stress and tension in the body.

Emotionally, an overactive Root Chakra can lead to an obsession with security and control. You may feel constantly worried about your financial situation, possessions, or physical safety, leading to feelings of anxiety, paranoia, or possessiveness. This heightened sense of fear and attachment can prevent you from fully experiencing life and trusting in the natural flow of events.

Mentally, an over-energised Root Chakra can manifest as rigidity, stubbornness, and resistance to change. You may cling to outdated beliefs, habits, or routines out of fear of losing stability or security. This resistance to growth and evolution can hinder your personal development and prevent you from embracing new opportunities for growth and expansion.

Overall, an overactive Root Chakra can disrupt your sense of balance, flexibility, and openness to life's experiences. Practices that promote grounding, relaxation, and release can help to channel this excess energy and restore harmony to the Root Chakra, allowing you to feel more secure, stable, and at peace within yourself and the world around you.

Food:

To balance the Root Chakra, it's beneficial to consume grounding foods that are nourishing and provide stability. Here are some suggestions for foods that can help balance the Root Chakra:

1. Root Vegetables - Incorporate root vegetables such as carrots, potatoes, sweet potatoes, beets, and onions into your diet. These vegetables grow underground, connecting us to the earth and providing a sense of grounding energy.
2. Protein-rich Foods - Include protein-rich foods like beans, lentils, chickpeas, tofu, tempeh, and lean meats. Protein helps to stabilise blood sugar levels and provides a sense of strength and vitality.
3. Red Foods - The Root Chakra is associated with the colour red, so consuming red foods can help balance this energy centre. Enjoy foods like red apples, strawberries, raspberries, cherries, tomatoes, beetroot and red peppers.
4. Earthy Grains - Opt for whole grains such as brown rice, quinoa, oats, and barley. These grains are nourishing and grounding, providing a steady source of energy.
5. Nuts and Seeds - Incorporate nuts and seeds such as almonds, walnuts, pumpkin seeds, and chia seeds into your diet. These foods are rich in nutrients, healthy fats, and fibre, promoting feelings of stability and security.

6. Spices - Use warming spices like ginger, turmeric, cinnamon, and cumin in your cooking. These spices help to stimulate digestion, improve circulation, and provide a sense of warmth and comfort.
7. Herbal Teas - Enjoy herbal teas made from roots such as ginger, liquorice, and dandelion root. These teas are soothing and grounding, promoting relaxation and balance in the Root Chakra.

By incorporating these nourishing foods into your diet, you can help balance and strengthen the Root Chakra, promoting a greater sense of stability, security, and connection to the earth.

When using crystals to balance the Root Chakra, you can place them near the base of your spine during meditation, carry them with you throughout the day, or incorporate them into your environment as decorative pieces. Allow yourself to connect with the energy of the crystals and set intentions for grounding, stability, and security.

By assessing these key points, you can gain insight into the state of your Root Chakra and identify areas that may require attention and healing. This awareness can guide you in implementing holistic practices to support the balancing and strengthening of your Root Chakra, fostering a greater sense of stability, security, and groundedness in your life.

Yoga Poses:

Yoga poses that focus on grounding, stability, and connecting with the lower body can help balance the Root Chakra. Here are some yoga poses specifically beneficial for balancing the Root Chakra (Muladhara):

1. Mountain Pose (Tadasana) - Stand tall with feet hip-width apart, grounding firmly into the earth. Feel the connection between your feet and the ground, engaging the muscles of the legs and the core. Lift through the crown of the head and lengthen the spine, cultivating a sense of stability and rootedness.

2. Tree Pose (Vrksasana) - Shift your weight onto one leg and lift the opposite foot, placing the sole against the inner thigh or calf of the standing leg. Press the foot into the thigh or calf, and the thigh or calf into the foot, finding balance and stability. Bring your hands to the heart in the centre or extend them overhead, focusing on a steady gaze to enhance concentration and grounding

3. Warrior I (Virabhadrasana I) - Step one foot back into a lunge position, with the front knee bent at a 90-degree angle and the back leg straight. Ground the outer edge of the back foot into the mat as you reach the arms overhead, lifting through the torso and engaging the core. Feel the strength and stability in the legs as you connect with the earth beneath you.

4. Bridge Pose (Setu Bandhasana) - Lie on your back with knees bent and feet hip-width apart, arms by your sides. Press into the feet to lift the hips towards the sky, creating a bridge shape with the body. Ground down through the feet and shoulders while lifting the pelvis, opening the heart and stimulating the Root Chakra.

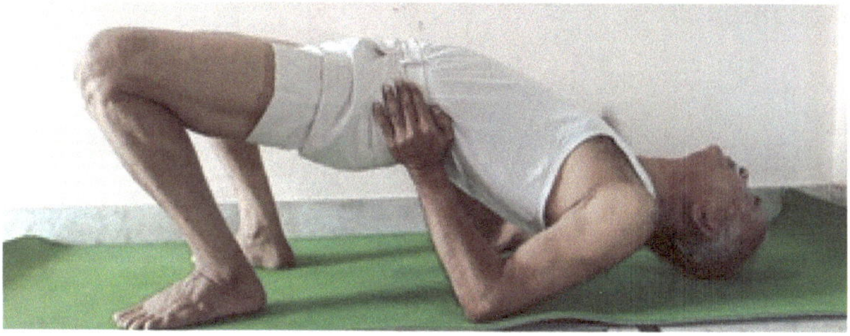

5. Child's Pose (Balasana) - Bend on your hands and knees, then sit back on your heels as you reach the arms forward and lower the forehead to the mat. Allow the hips to sink towards the heels while maintaining length through the spine. This gentle, resting pose promotes a sense of surrender and security, encouraging grounding and relaxation.

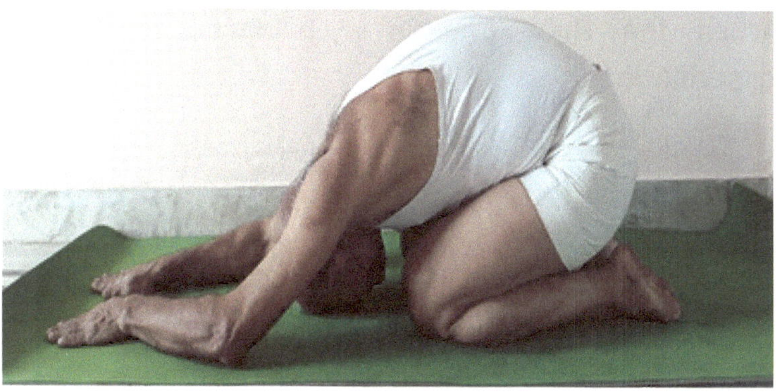

Practising these yoga poses mindfully and with awareness of the connection to the earth can help to balance and strengthen the Root Chakra, fostering a greater sense of stability, security, and groundedness in your body and mind.

Activities:

- Dance to your favourite music for 2 minutes.
- Perform body movements and stretching exercises.
- Go for a 15-minute uphill hike or mountain climbing.
- Engage in 1 minute of spot running.
- Spend 5 minutes gardening, watering plants, touching plants, and feeling the soil or earth.
- Take a conscious walk outside for 5-10 minutes, feeling the air and earth beneath your feet (consider going barefoot) without any phone calls.
- Sit on the floor and sense your hips for 1 minute.
- Use a ball to press under your feet and rotate it.

When the Root Chakra is balanced, individuals experience:

1. Focus and presence
2. Feeling stable and secure
3. A healthy survival instinct
4. Reliability
5. Responsibility

6. A sense of belonging
7. Feeling grounded
8. Connectedness to self and others
9. The ability to care for oneself
10. The drive to live.

Here are ten affirmations specifically tailored for the Root Chakra:

1. "I am grounded, stable, and secure in my life.'
2. "I trust in the abundance of the universe to provide for my needs."
3. "I am rooted deeply in the present moment, connected to the earth."
4. "I am safe and protected, surrounded by love and support."
5. "I release fear and embrace the flow of life with confidence."
6. "I honour my body as a sacred vessel and treat it with respect and care."
7. "I am worthy of love, success, and abundance in all areas of my life."
8. "I trust my intuition to guide me on my path towards growth and fulfilment."
9. I am empowered to create the life I desire with courage and determination.

10. "I am grateful for the gift of life and all the experiences it brings me."

These affirmations can help to reinforce positive beliefs and qualities associated with a balanced Root Chakra, promoting a sense of security, stability, and groundedness in your life.

Guided meditations and workshops are available in the Aj Life Mastery portal. www.ajlifemastery.com

CHAPTER 2

SACRAL CHAKRA (SWADHISTHANA)

The Sacral Chakra, located in the lower abdomen, governs emotions, creativity, and sexuality. It influences pleasure, passion, and the ability to experience joy in life. When balanced, it fosters emotional stability, creativity, and healthy relationships. Imbalances may manifest as emotional instability, creative blockages, or issues with intimacy and sexuality. To balance the Sacral Chakra, one can engage in activities that promote emotional expression, creative outlets, and healthy sensuality. This includes meditation, movement practices, artistic endeavours, and exploring one's passions. A balanced Sacral Chakra enhances overall well-being, fostering a deep sense of pleasure, fulfilment, and vitality in life.

- Location For Woman - Womb
- Location For Man - Between genitals
- Element - Water
- Colour - Orange
- Sound – Vam
- Gland - Ovaries and testicles

- Crystal – Sunstone, Carnelian, Tiger's Eye, Goldstone, Sunstone
- Aroma - Orange, Sandalwood, Patchouli, Jasmine, Neroli, Vanilla, Cinnamon, Ginger, Bergamot
- These glands are responsible for producing reproductive hormones such as oestrogen and testosterone
- Sense – Taste
- Deals with — Change, emotions, feelings, desires, polarities, nurturance, pleasure, sexuality

Characteristics of the Sacral Chakra:

The Sacral Chakra, also known as Svadhisthana in Sanskrit, is the second primary chakra located in the lower abdomen, just below the navel. It is associated with various aspects of human experience and plays a significant role in our emotional and creative expression, pleasure, and relationships. Here are some key significances of the Sacral Chakra:

1. Emotional Balance - The Sacral Chakra governs our emotions and feelings, including pleasure, joy, desire, and intimacy. When balanced, it promotes emotional stability, creativity, and healthy expression of emotions.
2. Creativity - This chakra is closely linked to creativity and the flow of creative energy. When balanced,

it allows for the free flow of ideas, inspiration, and artistic expression.

3. Sensuality and Sexuality - The Sacral Chakra is associated with sensuality, sexuality, and pleasure. It governs our ability to enjoy physical experiences and intimate connections with others.
4. Passion and Desire - It is the centre of our passion, desires, and drives in life. A balanced Sacral Chakra encourages enthusiasm, motivation, and a zest for life.
5. Relationships - This chakra influences our relationships with others, including romantic partnerships, friendships, and familial connections. It governs our ability to form healthy, balanced relationships based on mutual respect and emotional intimacy.
6. Self-Expression - The Sacral Chakra facilitates self-expression and communication, allowing us to express our feelings, desires, and needs openly and authentically.
7. Movement and Flow - It is associated with the element of water, symbolising the fluidity, adaptability, and movement in our lives. A balanced Sacral Chakra enables us to go with the flow and embrace change with grace.
8. Pleasure and Enjoyment - This chakra encourages us to seek and appreciate pleasure in all areas of life,

including food, music, art, and nature.

9. Manifestation - The Sacral Chakra plays a role in manifesting our desires and intentions into reality. When balanced, it supports our ability to attract abundance and create the life we desire.
10. Sacred Feminine - In many spiritual traditions, the Sacral Chakra is associated with the divine feminine energy, nurturing, and creativity.
11. Movement – Engage in physical activity or consider changing your environment.
12. Embrace Change – Transitioning from a frozen state to embracing the modern world.
13. Polarities – Experiencing attraction to the opposite sex, such as receiving marriage proposals.
14. Seek Pleasure – Find joy in dressing up, enjoying delicious food, and nurturing relationships.
15. Navigate Emotions – From highs to lows, allow yourself to release pain and embrace pleasure, as emotions drive desires, leading to movement and change.
16. Explore Sexuality – Foster healthy relationships and connections with partners.
17. Develop Clairsentience – Cultivate clear feelings and psychic senses, such as a mother's intuition or sensing others' moods in a crowd.
18. Practice Nurturance – Show tenderness, love, and

care through cuddling and physical touch, fostering emotional stability and connection.

Overall, the Sacral Chakra holds immense significance in our overall well-being, influencing our emotional, creative, and relational aspects of life. Balancing this chakra is essential for cultivating joy, fulfilment, and healthy relationships.

Self-test:

Answer in Yes or No

1. How would you rate your ability to feel and express emotions?
2. How would you rate your sex life?
3. How much time do you create for simple pleasures in your life?
4. How would you rate your physical flexibility?
5. How would you rate your emotional flexibility?
6. Are you able to nurture or be nurtured by others in balance?
7. Do you struggle with guilt about your feelings of sexuality?

N = Never P = Poor G= Good E =Excellent

Give points N & P =1, G = 2 and E = 3

Calculate and check out of 21 how many points you got Ex: 10/21

Let us work on balancing the Sacral Chakra

If blocked:

The Sacral Chakra, associated with emotions, creativity, and relationships, can significantly impact our emotional well-being. Here are the top five emotional impacts associated with the Sacral Chakra:

Emotional Impacts:

1. Emotional Instability - When the Sacral Chakra is imbalanced, individuals may experience emotional instability, mood swings, or difficulty regulating their feelings. This can manifest as periods of intense emotions followed by emotional numbness or disconnection.
2. Low Self-Esteem - The Sacral Chakra governs our sense of self-worth and confidence. Imbalances in this chakra can lead to feelings of inadequacy, self-doubt, or low self-esteem. Individuals may struggle to assert themselves or express their needs and desires in relationships.
3. Creativity Blocks - The Sacral Chakra is closely linked to creativity and self-expression. When imbalanced, individuals may experience creative blocks, lack of inspiration, or difficulty tapping into their creative potential. This can lead to feelings of frustration, stagnation, or unfulfilled creative potential.

4. Sexual Issues - The Sacral Chakra is also associated with sexuality, pleasure, and intimacy. Imbalances in this chakra can manifest as sexual issues such as low libido, lack of sexual satisfaction, or difficulties in forming intimate connections with others. Individuals may struggle with expressing their sexuality or experiencing pleasure in relationships.
5. Relationship Challenges - Imbalances in the Sacral Chakra can impact relationships by affecting our ability to connect emotionally and form healthy bonds with others. This can lead to relationship challenges such as co-dependency, fear of intimacy, or difficulty establishing boundaries. Individuals may struggle with trust issues, emotional intimacy, or maintaining healthy relationships.

Addressing imbalances in the Sacral Chakra through practices such as meditation, energy healing, creative expression, and emotional processing can help restore emotional balance and promote overall well-being. Therapy, self-reflection, and communication skills training can also provide valuable support in navigating emotional challenges associated with Sacral Chakra imbalances.

Relationship Impacts:

The Sacral Chakra, associated with emotions, creativity, and sexuality, plays a significant role in relationships. Here are the top five relationship impacts associated with the Sacral Chakra:

1. Intimacy and Connection - A balanced Sacral Chakra fosters intimacy and emotional connection in relationships. Individuals with a balanced Sacral Chakra are more open to expressing their emotions, desires, and vulnerabilities, leading to deeper and more fulfilling connections with their partners.
2. Passion and Sensuality - The Sacral Chakra is closely linked to sexuality, pleasure, and sensuality. When balanced, individuals experience heightened passion and enjoyment in their relationships, leading to greater satisfaction and intimacy in sexual interactions.
3. Creativity and Shared Activities - The Sacral Chakra governs creativity and self-expression. Couples with balanced Sacral Chakras often engage in creative and enjoyable activities together, such as art, music, dancing, or other forms of self-expression. This fosters a sense of shared joy and connection in the relationship.
4. Boundaries and Self-Worth - The Sacral Chakra influences self-esteem and the ability to set healthy boundaries in relationships. Individuals with balanced Sacral Chakras have a strong sense of self-worth and are better able to assert their needs and boundaries within the relationship, leading to mutual respect and understanding between partners.
5. Emotional Balance and Stability - Imbalances in the Sacral Chakra can lead to emotional instability and mood swings, which can impact the dynamics of a relationship. Couples may experience conflicts or

misunderstandings when one or both partners are unable to regulate their emotions effectively. Balancing the Sacral Chakra promotes emotional stability and harmony within the relationship.

Addressing imbalances in the Sacral Chakra through practices such as meditation, energy healing, creative expression, and self-reflection can help improve relationship dynamics and foster greater intimacy, passion, and emotional connection between partners. Couples therapy and communication skills training can also provide valuable support in navigating relationship challenges associated with Sacral Chakra imbalances.

Physical Impacts:

1. Reproductive Health - The Sacral Chakra is closely linked to the reproductive organs and reproductive health. Imbalances in this chakra may manifest as menstrual irregularities, fertility issues, or discomfort in the pelvic area.
2. Lower Abdomen - The area surrounding the Sacral Chakra, including the lower abdomen, pelvis, and hips, may experience discomfort, tension, or pain when the chakra is imbalanced.
3. Sexual Dysfunction - The Sacral Chakra governs sexuality and sexual energy. Imbalances in this chakra can lead to sexual dysfunction, such as erectile dysfunction or loss of libido, as well as difficulties in

experiencing pleasure or intimacy.

4. Digestive Problems - The Sacral Chakra is connected to the digestive system, particularly the lower abdomen. Imbalances in this chakra can lead to problems with the intestines and colon and digestive issues such as bloating, constipation, or abdominal discomfort.
5. Bladder and Kidney Health - The Sacral Chakra influences the urinary system, including the bladder and kidneys. Imbalances in this chakra may affect urinary function, leading to issues such as frequent urination, urinary tract infections, or kidney problems.
6. Immune System - The immune system may be compromised when the Sacral Chakra is imbalanced, making individuals more susceptible to infections, illnesses and autoimmune disorders.
7. Endocrine System - The Sacral Chakra influences the hormonal balance in the body, and imbalances may impact the function of the reproductive hormones, adrenal glands, and other endocrine organs.
8. Circulatory System - Imbalances in the Sacral Chakra can affect blood circulation, leading to issues such as poor circulation, cold hands and feet, or varicose veins.
9. Musculoskeletal System - Tension or imbalances in the Sacral Chakra may contribute to muscular tension, stiffness, or discomfort in the hips, pelvis, or lower back, along with disc bulges in the L4 and L5 vertebrae

of the spine, can lead to sciatica.

10. Nervous System - The Sacral Chakra is interconnected with the nervous system, and imbalances may contribute to symptoms such as fatigue, insomnia, or nervousness.

Overall, imbalances in the Sacral Chakra can manifest in various physical symptoms and affect different areas of the body, highlighting the importance of maintaining balance and harmony in this energy centre for overall well-being.

Addressing imbalances in the Sacral Chakra through practices such as meditation, energy healing, yoga, and bodywork can help alleviate physical symptoms and promote overall well-being. It's also important to seek medical attention for any persistent or severe physical symptoms to rule out underlying medical conditions.

If over energised:

If the Sacral Chakra is over-energised, individuals may experience various physical, emotional, and mental symptoms. Here are the top 10 signs of an over-energised Sacral Chakra:

1. Excessive Emotions - Intense and overwhelming emotions, including mood swings and heightened sensitivity.
2. Overindulgence - Compulsive behaviours such as overeating, overspending, or excessive consumption

of alcohol or drugs.

3. Hypersexuality - Obsessive thoughts or behaviours related to sex, leading to promiscuity or risky sexual behaviour.
4. Poor Boundaries - Difficulty setting boundaries with others, leading to codependent or enmeshed relationships.
5. Creative Blocks - Despite the abundance of energy, creativity may feel chaotic or stifled, leading to creative blocks or a lack of focus.
6. Emotional Instability - Fluctuating emotions and difficulty in maintaining emotional balance, leading to unpredictable behaviour.
7. Manipulative Behaviour - Using charm or manipulation to control or influence others for personal gain.
8. Guilt and Shame - Feeling overwhelmed by guilt or shame, especially relating to past actions or experiences.
9. Lack of Stability - Difficulty maintaining stability in relationships, finances, or other areas of life due to impulsivity or erratic behaviour.
10. Physical Symptoms - Physical manifestations such as lower back pain, reproductive issues, or urinary problems may arise due to the excessive energy in the Sacral Chakra.

It's important to address and balance the Sacral Chakra

to alleviate these symptoms and promote overall well-being. Practices such as meditation, yoga, journaling, and energy healing can help restore harmony to the Sacral Chakra.

When Balanced:

When the Sacral Chakra is balanced, individuals experience a variety of positive effects across different aspects of their lives:

1. Emotional Stability - A balanced Sacral Chakra promotes emotional stability, allowing individuals to navigate their feelings with ease and grace.
2. Creativity Flow - Creative energy flows freely, leading to increased inspiration, innovative thinking, and artistic expression.
3. Healthy Relationships - Individuals foster healthy, fulfilling relationships based on mutual respect, emotional intimacy, and genuine connection.
4. Sensuality and Pleasure - There is a heightened appreciation for sensual experiences, leading to greater enjoyment of life's pleasures and sensations.
5. Passion and Drive - Individuals feel motivated, enthusiastic, and driven to pursue their goals and desires with vigour and determination.
6. Positive Self-Expression - Self-expression becomes more authentic and uninhibited, allowing individuals

to communicate their thoughts, feelings, and desires openly and honestly.

7. Flexibility and Adaptability - There is an increased ability to adapt to change and go with the flow of life, embracing new experiences and challenges with ease.
8. Healthy Sexual Expression - Individuals experience a balanced and fulfilling sexuality, characterised by mutual pleasure, intimacy, and connection with partners.
9. Manifestation Power - The ability to manifest desires and intentions into reality is enhanced, leading to greater abundance and success in various areas of life.
10. Overall Well-Being - With the Sacral Chakra in balance, individuals experience a sense of overall well-being, joy, and vitality in their daily lives.

Balancing the Sacral Chakra is essential for cultivating a harmonious relationship with oneself and others, fostering creativity, and enhancing the overall quality of life.

Activities:

Activity 1 - Water meditation:

- Take a glass of water and drink slowly; feel the coolness till it hits your stomach.
- Imagine it passing through your veins, muscles

and digestive system.

- Wet your finger and rub it on your face - feel the coolness and refreshing quality.

Activity 2 – Bathing

- Take leisurely baths, allowing yourself to relax and unwind.
- If possible, visit beaches, lakes, and rivers, or enjoy a soak in a hot bathtub.
- When bathing, choose your favourite towel, soap, shampoo, and lotions to enhance the experience.
- Ensure the environment is clean and conducive to relaxation and rejuvenation.

Affirmations while Bathing:

- Become one with the water.
- Bless the water.
- Imagine it's Ganga water - Chant "Har Har Ganga".
- Say while pouring water on yourself to remove negative energy:

"My face is clear, my hands are clean, my feet are clean."

- Step back and feel the negative energy draining from your body.

- Feel the positive energy flow like a waterfall over you, filling your body.
- Dress yourself in clean clothes.
- Visiting a large body of water further softens the energy.

Masculine and Feminine - Ardhanarishwar

Masculine features encompass strength, assertiveness, logic, and action, while Feminine features embody nurturing, intuition, creativity, and receptivity.

When balanced within a person, Masculine and Feminine energies harmonise to create a holistic individual. This balance fosters inner peace, self-awareness, and emotional stability. It allows individuals to assert themselves confidently while also being receptive to others' needs.

Creativity flourishes alongside rationality, and relationships thrive on mutual respect and understanding.

Overall, a balanced integration of Masculine and Feminine features promotes personal growth, healthy relationships, and a sense of wholeness in one's being.

Expression: Masculine energy is often associated with qualities such as strength, assertiveness, and logic, while Feminine energy is associated with qualities like nurturing, intuition, and creativity. Both sets of qualities are essential for holistic self-expression and personal growth.

What if a Person Predominantly Embodies Masculine Traits?

If a person leans more towards Masculine energy, they may exhibit traits such as assertiveness, rationality, competitiveness, and a focus on action and achievement.

While these qualities can be beneficial in certain situations, an imbalance towards Masculine energy may lead to tendencies such as aggression, dominance, rigidity, and a lack of emotional expression or empathy.

It could also result in difficulty nurturing relationships or connecting with others on an emotional level.

To achieve greater balance, individuals leaning towards Masculine energy may benefit from cultivating qualities associated with Feminine energy, such as receptivity, intuition, creativity, and emotional sensitivity. This can lead to a more harmonious and holistic approach to life and relationships.

What if a Person Primarily Embodies Feminine Traits?

If a person primarily embodies Feminine traits, they may exhibit characteristics such as nurturing, empathy, intuition, creativity, and emotional sensitivity.

While these qualities can be advantageous in fostering connections, compassion, and creativity, an imbalance towards Feminine energy may also lead to challenges such as indecisiveness, passivity, and being overly accommodating.

Additionally, individuals may struggle with assertiveness or setting boundaries. To achieve greater balance, those leaning towards Feminine energy may benefit from cultivating qualities associated with Masculine energy, such as assertiveness, rationality, and action-oriented behaviour. This can promote a more balanced approach to life and relationships.

Food:

Some foods that are commonly associated with balancing the Sacral Chakra:

1. Orange Foods - Oranges, carrots, pumpkin, sweet potatoes; oranges are rich in nutrients and vibrant in colour, stimulating the Sacral Chakra.
2. Nuts and Seeds - Almonds, walnuts, pumpkin seeds, and sesame seeds are high in healthy fats and nutrients, supporting overall well-being and balance.
3. Sweet Fruits - Mangoes, papayas, oranges, and passion fruit are naturally sweet and refreshing, providing nourishment to the Sacral Chakra.
4. Honey - Honey is considered a natural sweetener that can help to balance the Sacral Chakra when consumed in moderation.
5. Spices - Cinnamon, ginger, and cardamom are warming spices that can stimulate the Sacral Chakra and enhance feelings of pleasure and sensuality.

6. Water - Staying hydrated with pure, clean water is essential for balancing all chakras, including the Sacral Chakra, as it promotes fluidity and flow in the body and mind.
7. Coconut - Coconut water, coconut milk, and coconut flesh are hydrating and nourishing, supporting the Sacral Chakra's energy of flow and abundance.
8. Herbal Teas: Chamomile, fennel, and ginger teas can help to calm the mind and soothe the emotions, promoting balance and harmony in the Sacral Chakra.
9. Seafood: Fresh fish, especially those rich in omega-3 fatty acids such as salmon and mackerel, are beneficial for the Sacral Chakra, as they promote feelings of well-being and emotional balance.
10. Root Vegetables: Root vegetables such as beets, carrots, and potatoes are grounding and nourishing, supporting the stability and vitality of the Sacral Chakra.

Incorporating these foods into your diet can help to nourish and balance the Sacral Chakra, promoting feelings of pleasure, creativity, and emotional well-being.

Creative Activities:

Dance, painting, drawing, mould pottery, long showers, salt water therapy.

Yoga poses:

1. Goddess pose (You can do this while lying down as well)

2. Butterfly position – stay still

3. Child pose

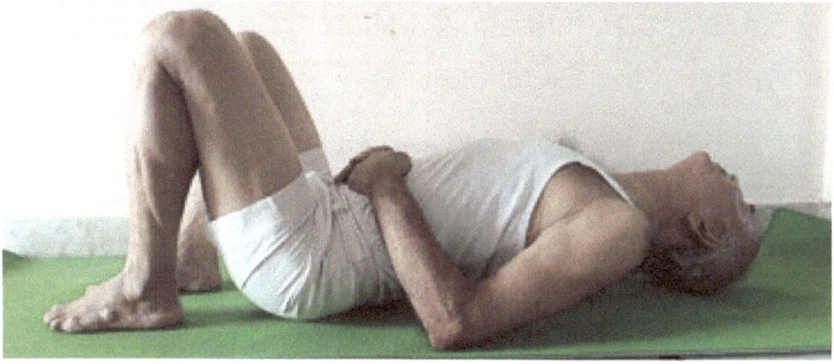

4. Pelvic Rock

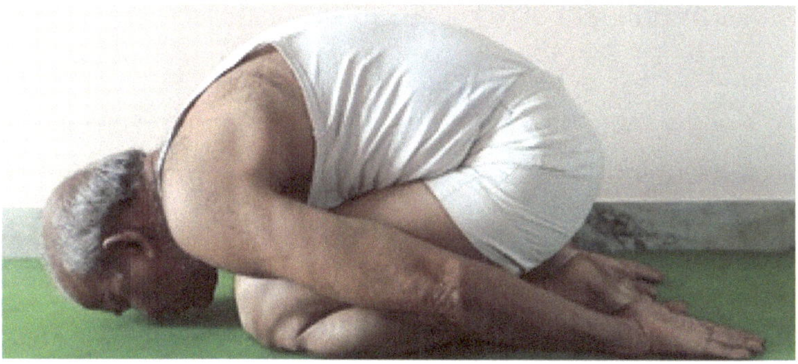

5. Scissors kicks

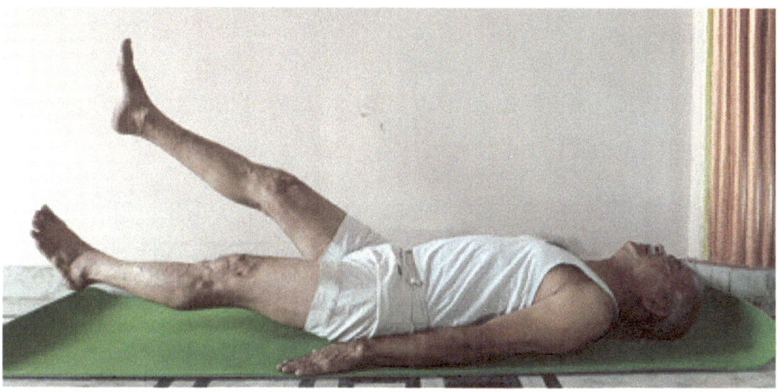

Affirmations:

Some of the affirmations to support the balancing and activation of the Sacral Chakra:

1. "I embrace pleasure and joy in all aspects of my life."
2. "My emotions are balanced, and I express them freely and authentically."
3. "I am worthy of love, creativity, and abundance."
4. "I honour my body as a sacred vessel of pleasure and creativity."
5. "I am confident of my sexuality and embrace my sensual nature."
6. "I allow myself to experience and express my emotions without judgment."
7. "I am open to receiving love, pleasure in abundance from the universe."
8. "I trust my intuition and follow its guidance with confidence."
9. "I am creative and inspired, and my ideas flow freely and effortlessly."
10. "I am connected to my inner power and harness it to create a fulfilling life."

Repeat these affirmations regularly, either silently or aloud, to reinforce positive beliefs and energies associated with the Sacral Chakra, promoting balance, vitality, and creativity in your life.

CHAPTER 3

SOLAR PLEXUS CHAKRA (MANIPURA)

The Solar Plexus Chakra, Manipura, located below the rib cage, embodies personal power and confidence. When balanced, it empowers clear decision-making and assertiveness. This radiant centre fosters self-esteem and authenticity, enabling one to stand firm in their uniqueness. Conversely, imbalance manifests as insecurity and indecision. To harmonise and nurture self-worth through boundary-setting and self-reflection. Engage in activities that ignite passion and embrace challenges for growth. Cultivate inner strength to manifest desires fearlessly. By honouring this chakra, individuals unlock their innate courage and determination, embracing life with authenticity and confidence.

- Location - stomach area, a couple of centimetres above the navel.
- Element - Fire
- Colour - Yellow
- Sound - RAM
- Gland – Pancreas, adrenals
- Crystals – Amber, Yellow Jasper, Yellow Tiger's Eye,

Citrine

- Aromas - Lemon, ginger, bergamot, chamomile, peppermint
- Solar Plexus Chakra is associated with the stomach, gallbladder, spleen, liver, and pancreas
- Governs your metabolism, and it is responsible for the regulation and distribution of metabolic energy throughout the body
- Sense - Sight
- It deals with power, will, autonomy, energy, metabolism, technology, transformation, and self-esteem.

Fire Meditation:

As this chakra deals with fire, let's engage in a fire meditation.

- Before beginning the fire meditation, light your favourite candle.
- Sit in a lotus pose with your spine straight, relax your body, and take a few deep breaths.
- Focus on the candle and envision the wick as your physical body and the flame as the energy radiating from your body into the Universe.
- Spend a couple of minutes breathing deeply and gazing at the image of the golden flame.
- Visualise yourself merging with the flame, becoming pure, universal light and energy.
- As you delve deeper into the meditation, gently shift your focus to your Solar Plexus Chakra and visualise a yellow ball of flame within this area.
- Imagine it growing warmer, expanding, and burning away all obstacles.
- Feel the power of fire within your body and visualise how it transforms your life, granting you infinite energy and strength.
- Remain in this powerful state for a few minutes to integrate this transformative energy.
- Conclude the meditation with words of gratitude, allowing this light to shine before you and empowering you to change your life.

Characteristics of the Solar Plexus Chakra:

The Solar Plexus Chakra, also known as Manipura, is associated with various characteristics that reflect its energy and influence. Here are ten key characteristics of the Solar Plexus Chakra:

1. Personal Power - The Solar Plexus Chakra governs our sense of personal power and autonomy, empowering us to assert ourselves confidently in the world.
2. Self-Esteem - It influences our self-esteem and self-worth, shaping how we perceive ourselves and our abilities.
3. Confidence - A balanced Solar Plexus Chakra fosters confidence and self-assurance, allowing us to tackle challenges with courage and conviction.
4. Willpower - This chakra is linked to our willpower and determination, enabling us to set and pursue goals with perseverance and resolve.
5. Inner Strength - It represents our inner strength and resilience, helping us navigate life's ups and downs with grace and resilience.
6. Emotional Stability - A harmonised Solar Plexus Chakra promotes emotional stability and balance, allowing us to manage our emotions effectively.
7. Personal Identity - It influences our sense of personal identity and individuality, supporting us in expressing our authentic selves without fear or hesitation.

8. Digestive Health - The Solar Plexus Chakra is associated with digestive organs and functions, affecting our digestion and metabolism.
9. Decision Making - It governs our ability to make decisions and choices confidently, guiding us towards paths that align with our true desires and intentions.
10. Empowerment - Ultimately, the Solar Plexus Chakra embodies empowerment, encouraging us to take ownership of our lives and pursue our dreams with passion and purpose.

These characteristics highlight the importance of maintaining balance and alignment in the Solar Plexus Chakra to cultivate a strong sense of self and navigate life's challenges with confidence and resilience.

Self-Test:

Answer in Yes or No

1. Do you feel a lack of energy and motivation?
2. Do you feel a lack of drive, determination, and direction in life?
3. Do you feel helpless?
4. Do you feel low self-esteem and low confidence?
5. Are you always seeking confirmation from others?
6. Are you always trying to fit in and please others?
7. Do you feel guilty and ashamed when you say "no" to people?

8. Do you often experience tiredness and fatigue?
9. Do you feel coldness in the Solar Plexus region?
10. Do you have a slow metabolism, or have obesity?

Results:

Check if your answer is Yes or No. If you get 'Yes' then see the results below;

8-10 – Excellent

5-7 – Good

2-4 – can be better

0-1 – Best of luck

If Blocked:

When the Solar Plexus Chakra is blocked or imbalanced, it can have various impacts on emotional, relational, and physical levels:

Emotional Impact:

1. Low Self-Confidence - A balanced Solar Plexus Chakra fosters self-confidence and a strong sense of self-worth. Individuals with a balanced Solar Plexus Chakra feel empowered to pursue their goals and assert themselves in various aspects of life.
2. Low Self-Esteem - The Solar Plexus Chakra influences self-esteem and self-respect. Imbalances in this chakra

can lead to low self-esteem, feelings of inadequacy, or a lack of confidence in one's abilities and worthiness.

3. Personal Power - The Solar Plexus Chakra is associated with personal power and autonomy. When balanced, individuals feel empowered to take control of their lives, make decisions, and assert their boundaries with confidence.
4. Emotional Regulation - Imbalances in the Solar Plexus Chakra can lead to difficulties in regulating emotions. Individuals may experience mood swings, irritability, or emotional volatility when this chakra is imbalanced.
5. Fear and Anxiety - The Solar Plexus Chakra is closely linked to our sense of identity and security. Imbalances in this chakra can lead to feelings of fear, anxiety, or insecurity about one's place in the world and ability to navigate life's challenges.
6. Anger and Frustration - Blocked energy in this chakra can manifest as unresolved anger or frustration, as individuals may feel powerless or unable to express their emotions assertively.

Relationship Impacts:

1. Power control - When feeling low in power and control, individuals may exhibit passive or submissive behaviour, avoiding confrontation and decision-making. They might seek approval from others, doubting their abilities and struggling to assert themselves. Indecision

and avoidance of challenges may be common, while some may overcompensate with aggressive or controlling tendencies. The fear of making mistakes and the burden of responsibility can lead to a sense of overwhelm.

2. Low Self-Esteem - An underactive Solar Plexus Chakra can result in low self-esteem and self-doubt, which may negatively impact relationships. Individuals may struggle to assert themselves, express their needs, or feel worthy of love and respect from their partners.
3. Co-dependency - Imbalances in the Solar Plexus Chakra can contribute to codependent relationships, where individuals overly rely on their partners for validation, approval, or a sense of identity. This can lead to unhealthy attachment patterns and emotional dependency.
4. Conflict Avoidance - Individuals with imbalanced Solar Plexus Chakras may avoid conflict or confrontation in relationships, fearing rejection or disapproval. This can lead to unresolved issues, pent-up emotions, and communication breakdowns, undermining the health and longevity of the relationship.
5. Lack of Boundaries - An imbalanced Solar Plexus Chakra can result in unclear or porous boundaries in relationships. Individuals may struggle to assert their boundaries, leading to feelings of resentment, frustration, or violation when their needs are not respected by their partners.

Physical Impacts:

Here are the physical impacts associated with an imbalanced Solar Plexus Chakra:

1. Digestive Issues - Imbalances in the Solar Plexus Chakra can disrupt the functioning of the digestive system, leading to problems such as indigestion, bloating, gas, constipation, or diarrhoea.
2. Abdominal Discomfort - Individuals with imbalanced Solar Plexus Chakras may experience discomfort or pain in the upper abdomen, including sensations of tightness, pressure, or cramping.
3. Nervous System Disorders - The Solar Plexus Chakra influences the autonomic nervous system, which regulates involuntary bodily functions. Imbalances in this chakra may contribute to conditions such as nervousness, anxiety, or stress-related disorders.
4. Muscular Tension - Imbalanced Solar Plexus Chakras can lead to muscular tension or stiffness in the abdomen, back, or shoulders. This tension may manifest as knots, tightness, or discomfort in the affected areas.
5. Fatigue - Individuals with imbalanced Solar Plexus Chakras may experience feelings of fatigue, lethargy, or lack of energy. This can result from disrupted energy flow in the chakra system, leading to a general sense of physical and mental exhaustion.

Mental Effects:

1. Indecision and lack of direction - A blocked Solar Plexus Chakra can lead to confusion and indecisiveness about one's goals and aspirations
2. Lack of Motivation - Individuals may struggle to find motivation and drive to pursue their passions or achieve their goals.
3. Feelings of Helplessness - There can be a sense of powerlessness and inability to take charge of one's life's circumstances.

Behavioural Patterns:

1. Perfectionism - Some individuals may develop perfectionistic tendencies as a way to compensate for feelings of inadequacy or lack of control.
2. Overcompensation or Aggression - In an attempt to assert themselves, individuals with a blocked Solar Plexus Chakra may exhibit aggressive or domineering behaviour.
3. Avoidance - People may avoid confrontational situations or challenges to maintain a sense of safety and control.

Overall, an imbalance in the Solar Plexus Chakra can have far-reaching effects on emotional, relational, and physical well-being, highlighting the importance of addressing and restoring balance in this energy centre through various healing practices and self-care techniques.

If Over Energised:

When the Solar Plexus Chakra is over-energised or excessively active, it can lead to imbalances and challenges on emotional, mental, and physical levels. Some manifestations of an overactive Solar Plexus Chakra include:

1. Dominance and Control - Individuals may exhibit domineering or controlling behaviour, seeking to assert their power and authority over others in relationships and situations.
2. Aggressiveness - There might be a tendency towards aggression, impulsivity, or anger, as the individual struggles to manage the heightened energy in the Solar Plexus Chakra.
3. Competitiveness - An overactive Solar Plexus Chakra may lead to excessive competitiveness, as individuals feel a constant need to prove themselves or outperform others.
4. Arrogance - There can be a sense of superiority or arrogance, with individuals feeling overly confident in their abilities and dismissive of others' perspectives.
5. Difficulty Listening - The heightened energy in the Solar Plexus Chakra may result in difficulty listening to others or considering alternative viewpoints, as the focus is primarily on asserting one's own opinions and desires.
6. Digestive Issues - Excessive energy in the Solar Plexus Chakra can manifest as digestive problems such as

acid reflux, ulcers, or irritable bowel syndrome due to heightened stress and tension.

7. Burnout - Constantly operating in a state of high energy and intensity can lead to burnout and exhaustion, both physically and mentally.
8. Impatience - There may be a lack of patience and tolerance for delays or setbacks, as individuals feel driven to achieve their goals quickly and assert their dominance.

To address an overactive Solar Plexus Chakra, it's important to focus on practices that promote balance and harmony, such as mindfulness, meditation, grounding exercises, and activities that encourage empathy and compassion towards others. It's also essential to cultivate self - awareness and recognise when assertiveness crosses over into aggression, striving for a healthy balance of personal power and humility.

Food:

The Solar Plexus Chakra is associated with the element of fire and is linked to personal power, confidence, and self-esteem. Therefore, the best foods to support the Solar Plexus Chakra are those that are energetically aligned with these qualities and promote vitality and balance. Some examples include:

1. Whole Grains - Whole grains like brown rice, quinoa, and oats provide sustained energy and help stabilise blood sugar levels, supporting mental clarity and focus.

2. Yellow Fruits and Vegetables - Yellow-coloured foods such as bananas, lemons, yellow bell peppers, and yellow squash are associated with the Solar Plexus Chakra. They are rich in antioxidants, vitamins, and minerals that promote digestion and metabolism.

3. Spices - Spices like ginger, turmeric, cumin, and cinnamon have warming properties that stimulate digestion and support the fire element of the Solar Plexus Chakra.

4. Healthy Fats - Foods rich in healthy fats, such as avocados, nuts, seeds, and olive oil, provide sustained energy and support brain health, enhancing mental clarity and confidence.

5. Legumes - Legumes like lentils, chickpeas, and beans are high in protein and fibre, promoting digestive health and providing long-lasting energy.

6. Herbal Teas - Herbal teas like chamomile, peppermint, and ginger tea can help soothe the digestive system, reduce stress, and promote relaxation, supporting overall balance in the Solar Plexus Chakra.

7. Sunflower Seeds - Sunflower seeds are rich in nutrients like vitamin E, magnesium, and selenium, which support overall vitality and energy levels.

8. Foods Rich in Vitamin C - Vitamin C-rich foods like oranges, grapefruits, strawberries, and kiwi help boost immunity and support the body's natural detoxification processes, promoting overall health and well-being.

Incorporating these foods into your diet can help support the balance and vitality of the Solar Plexus Chakra, enhancing feelings of personal power, confidence, and self-esteem.

Yoga Poses:

1. Wood Chopper - Make the sound "ha" while going down.

2. Pike

3. Planks

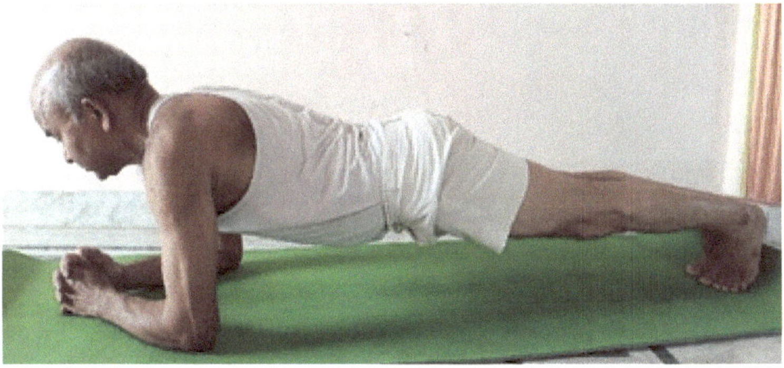

4. Surya Namaskara

5. Bow Pose

What are Cords?

Cord connections between people in the universe refer to energetic ties formed through interactions, emotions, and experiences. These cords, often metaphorical, represent the exchange of energy between individuals, influencing thoughts, feelings, and behaviours. Positive connections foster love, support, and growth, while negative ones may drain energy or create unhealthy attachments. Awareness and intentions are key to managing these cords, as maintaining healthy boundaries and nurturing positive relationships can enhance well-being and promote harmony in the interconnected web of human connections within the universe.

Activity:

Cutting cords involves severing energetic ties between individuals, freeing oneself from unhealthy attachments or negative influences. Here's a step-by-step guide:

1. Intention Setting - Set a clear intention to release any energetic cords that no longer serve your best interest.
2. Visualisation - Close your eyes and visualise the cords connecting you to the other person. See them clearly in your mind's eye.
3. Symbolic Action - Envision a sharp, shining tool such as a sword, scissors, or light cutting through the cords with precision.
4. Declaration - Verbally declare your intention to cut the cords. You can say something like, "I now release and cut all energetic cords that no longer serve my best interest."
5. Cutting Motion - Mentally or physically, make a cutting motion, severing the cords one by one. Visualise them

dissolving into light and returning to the universe.

PS: Call upon the deity you feel comfortable with, like Goddess Durga or Archangel Michael, to cut the cord in your mind.

6. Cleansing - Visualise a healing light washing over you, cleansing any residual energy and filling you with positivity and strength.
7. Protection - Surround yourself with a protective bubble of light or imagine yourself enveloped in a cloak of divine protection, shielding you from further attachment.
8. Gratitude - Express gratitude for the lessons learned and the growth achieved through the connection, acknowledging that it's time to move forward independently.

Repeat this process as needed, especially after significant interactions or when feeling energetically drained. It's essential to remember that cutting cords is a personal empowerment practice and not an act of severing relationships. It's about releasing attachments and reclaiming your own energy and autonomy.

When Balanced:

When the Solar Plexus Chakra is balanced, it results in several positive effects on emotional, mental, and physical levels:

1. Confidence - You feel confident in yourself and your abilities, allowing you to assert yourself with ease in various situations.
2. Self-Esteem - Your self-esteem is strong, and you have a healthy sense of self-worth and self-respect.
3. Personal Power - You feel empowered and in control of your life, able to make decisions and take action with clarity and purpose.
4. Motivation - You are motivated and driven to pursue your goals and aspirations with a clear sense of direction and purpose.
5. Emotional Stability - Your emotions are balanced, and you can manage stress, anxiety, and other emotions effectively.
6. Healthy Boundaries - You establish and maintain healthy boundaries in relationships, ensuring that your needs are met while respecting the needs of others.
7. Digestive Health - Your digestive system functions well, and you experience fewer digestive issues such as indigestion or bloating.
8. Vitality - You feel energised and vital, with a strong sense of inner vitality and resilience.

Your Solar Plexus Chakra will open up as soon as you begin to understand your place in the world and move towards a healthy self-image with full confidence. This process requires developing self-awareness, self-love, and fully accepting who you are in the present moment.

When your Solar Plexus Chakra opens up, you will finally understand how to use your personal power to bring your biggest gifts into this world. At that moment, you will stop living in a competitive state of mind and understand the true meaning of collaboration and abundance.

Overall, a balanced Solar Plexus Chakra results in a strong sense of self-confidence, personal power, and emotional stability, enabling you to navigate life with courage, clarity, and resilience.

Affirmations:

Affirmations specifically tailored to balance and empower the Solar Plexus Chakra:

1. "I am confident in my abilities and trust myself to make the right decisions."
2. "I honour and respect myself, recognising my inherent worth and value."
3. "I embrace my personal power and use it wisely to manifest my goals."
4. "I stand tall in my authenticity, expressing myself with courage and conviction."
5. "I am worthy of success, abundance, and all the good things life has to offer."
6. "I embrace challenges as opportunities for growth and transformation."
7. "I release fear and insecurity, replacing them with self-

assurance and inner strength."

8. "I am in control of my life and create my own reality with intention and purpose".
9. "I honour my unique talents and gifts, sharing them confidently with the world."
10. "I radiate confidence, vitality, and positive energy, attracting success and prosperity into my life."

Repeat these affirmations regularly, focusing on your Solar Plexus Chakra, to promote balance, confidence, and empowerment in this energy centre.

CHAPTER 4

HEART CHAKRA (ANAHATA)

The Heart Chakra, Anahata, is the fourth chakra located at the centre of the chest. It symbolises love, compassion, and connection. A balanced Heart Chakra fosters empathy, forgiveness, and harmonious relationships. Individuals experience unconditional love, embracing vulnerability and authenticity. Imbalances can lead to jealousy, resentment, or fear of intimacy. Physically, heart-related ailments and respiratory issues may arise. Practices like meditation, yoga, and acts of kindness help balance the Heart Chakra, fostering healing and alignment. Cultivating love and compassion towards oneself and others is essential for maintaining harmony in the Heart Chakra.

- Location - Heart
- Element - Air
- Colour - Green
- Sound - Yam
- Gland – Thymus
- Crystals - Green aventurine, emerald, jade, rose quartz

- Aroma - Rose
- Produce a variety of hormones such as adrenaline, steroids, aldosterone and cortisol.
- Their functions include the regulation of metabolism and the immune system.
- Sense - Touch
- Deals with asthma, high blood pressure, heart and lung diseases

Characteristics of the Heart Chakra:

When the Heart Chakra is balanced, one experiences a profound sense of love and interconnectedness with oneself, others, and the universe. Individuals feel compassion towards themselves and others, fostering harmonious relationships and empathy towards all beings. An open Heart Chakra allows for forgiveness, healing, and unconditional love, enabling individuals to embrace vulnerability and authenticity.

However, imbalances in the Heart Chakra can lead to emotional issues such as jealousy, resentment, or a fear of intimacy. Physical manifestations may include heart-related ailments, respiratory problems, or immune system disorders.

To balance the Heart Chakra, various practices such as meditation, yoga, deep breathing exercises, and acts of kindness can be employed. Surrounding oneself with nature, practising gratitude, and engaging in heart-opening activities like volunteering or spending time with loved ones can also foster healing and alignment in the Heart Chakra. Ultimately, cultivating love and compassion towards oneself and others is key to maintaining balance and harmony in the Heart Chakra.

Self-Test:

Answer in Yes or No

1. Do you share? e.g. Food, things, advice, knowledge, results in growth and fulfilment?
2. Are you focused on pure love and life balancing (instead of having everything; money, health, relationships etc.)?
3. Are you focused on spiritual balancing?
4. Do you forgive others? Maybe not straight away, but later?
5. How is your breathing? Is it normal, shallow or deep?
6. Do you like to spread joy and love? Do contributions and praise feel good from the inside when you share happiness and love?
7. Are you happy to give love? Like helping others financially or lending your hand?
8. Are you friendly and compassionate?
9. Do you accept yourself for who you are?
10. Do you easily say yes to people in general?

11. Do you feel grateful for whatever you have?
12. Can you say NO to people without guilt when needed?

Results:

Check if your answer is Yes or No. If you get 'Yes' then see the results below;

8-12 – Excellent

5-7 – Good

2-4 – Can be better

0-1 – Best of luck

If Blocked:

When the Heart Chakra is blocked, it can have significant impacts on emotional, relational, and physical levels:

Emotional Impacts:

1. Difficulty expressing or receiving love and affection, leading to feelings of loneliness or isolation.
2. Inability to forgive oneself or others, resulting in unresolved feelings of anger, resentment, or bitterness.
3. Suppressed emotions lead to emotional numbness or a sense of being disconnected from one's feelings.
4. Increased vulnerability to mood swings, anxiety, or depression due to unresolved emotional pain.

5. Lack of empathy and compassion towards oneself and others, resulting in a lack of emotional connection and understanding.

Relationship Impacts:

1. Difficulty forming or maintaining healthy relationships due to fear of intimacy or vulnerability.
2. Strained relationships are characterised by mistrust, jealousy, or co-dependency.
3. Inability to communicate openly and honestly with others, leading to misunderstandings or conflicts.
4. Feelings of isolation or disconnection in relationships, even with loved ones.

Physical Impacts:

1. Chest pain or tightness, heart palpitations, or other cardiovascular issues.
2. Respiratory issues such as asthma or shortness of breath.
3. Immune system disorders or chronic illnesses due to stress and emotional imbalance.
4. Digestive issues such as indigestion or stomach ulcers due to emotional stress impact the digestive system.

Overall, a blocked Heart Chakra can significantly impact emotional well-being, relationships, and physical health.

Addressing and healing the blockage through practices such as meditation, yoga, forgiveness, and self-love is essential for restoring balance and harmony in all aspects of life.

Addressing and healing a blocked Heart Chakra involves practices such as meditation, yoga, breathwork, forgiveness exercises, and engaging in acts of love and kindness towards oneself and others.

If Over Energised:

When the Heart Chakra is over-energised or excessively active, it can lead to imbalances and challenges on emotional, relational, and physical levels:

1. Overwhelming relationships - Excessive energy in the Heart Chakra may lead to becoming overly emotionally invested in relationships, resulting in co-dependency or smothering behaviour.
2. Boundary issues - There may be a lack of healthy boundaries in relationships, leading to difficulties in discerning one's own needs and desires from those of others.
3. Emotional instability - Overstimulation of the Heart Chakra can result in heightened emotional sensitivity, leading to mood swings, emotional outbursts, or irrational behaviour.
4. Giving too much - Individuals with an overactive Heart Chakra may prioritise others' needs over their

own, neglecting self-care and leading to burnout or resentment.

5. Difficulty letting go - There may be a tendency to hold onto past hurts or cling to relationships even when they are no longer serving one's best interest.
6. People-pleasing - Individuals may excessively seek validation and approval from others, compromising their authenticity and sense of self.
7. Unhealthy attachments - Over-energising the Heart Chakra can lead to attachment issues, including possessiveness or jealousy in relationships.
8. Physical symptoms - Physical manifestations of an overactive Heart Chakra may include heart palpitations, chest pain, or respiratory issues.
9. Emotional exhaustion - Constantly giving and overextending oneself in relationships can lead to emotional exhaustion and depletion.
10. Lack of self-love - Despite outwardly caring for others, individuals with an overactive Heart Chakra may struggle with self-love and self-acceptance, seeking external validation to fill an internal void.

It's important to balance and harmonise the Heart Chakra through practices such as meditation, mindfulness, setting healthy boundaries, and fostering self-love to avoid the negative effects of overstimulation.

Food:

Foods suggested to balance the Heart Chakra are those that promote feelings of love, compassion, and connection. Here are some examples:

1. Leafy greens - Spinach, kale, and Swiss chard are rich in nutrients and antioxidants that support heart health and overall well-being.
2. Green vegetables - Broccoli, green beans, and zucchini are also excellent choices as they help nourish the Heart Chakra and promote vitality.
3. Green fruits - Avocado, kiwi, and green apples are high in vitamins, minerals, and fibre, supporting heart health and emotional balance.
4. Green tea - Known for its calming properties, green tea can help soothe the heart and promote relaxation.
5. Berries - Blueberries, strawberries, and raspberries are rich in antioxidants and promote feelings of love and connection.
6. Nuts and seeds - Almonds, walnuts, and chia seeds are high in heart-healthy fats, protein, and fibre, supporting overall well- being.
7. Healthy fats - Olive oil, coconut oil, and fatty fish, like salmon are rich in omega-3 fatty acids, which support heart health and emotional balance.
8. Herbal teas - Chamomile, hibiscus, and rose tea can help calm the mind and promote feelings of love and

connection.

9. Foods with vibrant colours - Eating a variety of colourful fruits and vegetables can help balance the Heart Chakra and promote overall health and vitality.
10. Foods cooked with love - Cooking and sharing meals with loved ones can also help nourish the Heart Chakra and promote emotional well-being.

Unconditional Love:

Self-Love

First Love - Mother and child, partners, love for God.

Rejection - Non-love, self-destruction, separation, isolation, abandonment.

Feelings of Risk - Opening up, sharing, feeling. Restriction - Upper and lower chakras are blocked as well.

Love is at our core, our power, our centre, and the reason for our existence.

Moreover, love is a sense of spiritual connection, a sense of being touched, and can bring about change that pushes us beyond our limits.

Caring, nurturing, and feeling protected. Relationships and family: Acceptance:

Why does this generation experience more breakups and divorces? There are many reasons, but the top three are:

1. Upbringing - Family environment, including parents, relatives, society, and schooling, plays a significant role.
2. Helplessness - Many individuals are unable to explore the world and seek a partner to provide them the happiness they missed in their lives. It's important to remember that "you attract what you think." Negativity attracts negative partners who may be in similar situations.

Solution - Get married after achieving success and finding joy so you attract someone in a similar positive state.

3. Masculine and feminine - For instance, a girl brought up as a boy may later reject her feminine side and adopt a tomboy persona. This can result in physical issues such as PCOD problems and the growth of facial hair on the chin. Additionally, it may lead to life challenges such as difficulty in finding the right partner, which could ultimately result in divorce.

Solution - Accept who you are.

Activities:

1. Pranayam (Anulom Vilom)

2. Play with children (energy transformation) exchange of love and satisfaction.

3. Sit alone and feel the open air.
4. Meditative, deep breathing (hold and release slowly)
5. Rest beside the open window. (observe things outside the window)

Activity 1: Inhale and exhale through an open mouth (inhale through the nose and exhale through the mouth).

This activity helps alleviate physical ailments such as gastric issues, nausea, physical discomfort, and acidity.

Activity 2: The power within you - You become what you think.

To grow your finger, follow the steps below:

1. Align both hands so that the palm lines are equal, and bring them together in the Namaste position. Observe that one of the middle fingers is larger than the other hand's middle finger.
2. Now, open your hands and mentally command the smaller middle finger hand to grow eight times.
3. Join both hands together again and observe that the middle fingers of both hands are now the same size.
4. Repeat the above steps and mentally command the middle finger to return to its normal size; it will naturally revert to its usual state.

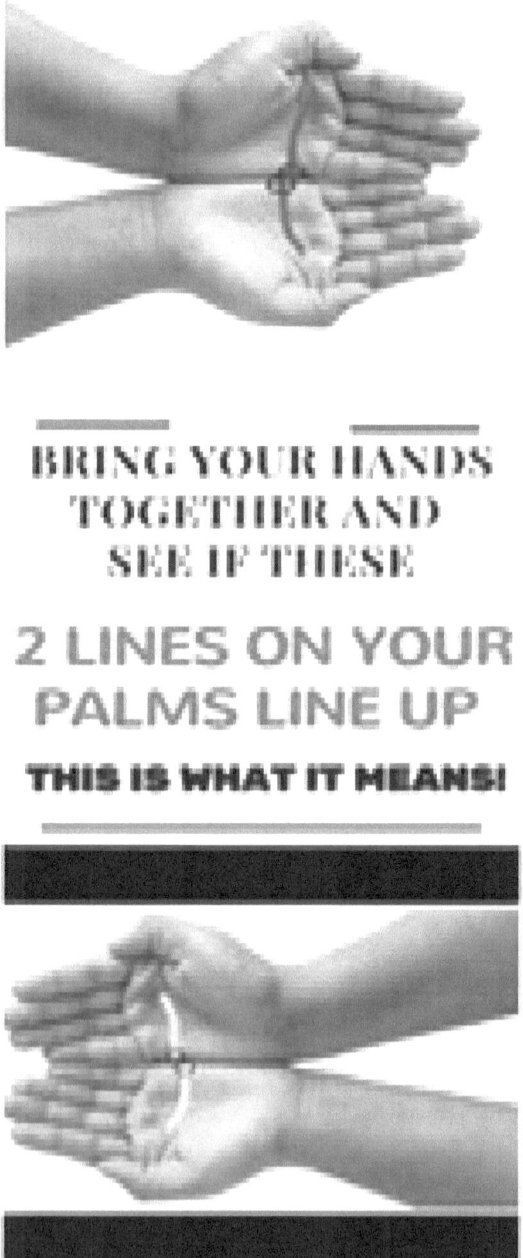
BRING YOUR HANDS
TOGETHER AND
SEE IF THESE
2 LINES ON YOUR
PALMS LINE UP
THIS IS WHAT IT MEANS!

Yoga poses:

1. Superman Pose

2. Cobra Position

3. Chest Opener

4. Baby Sleep Position on Stomach

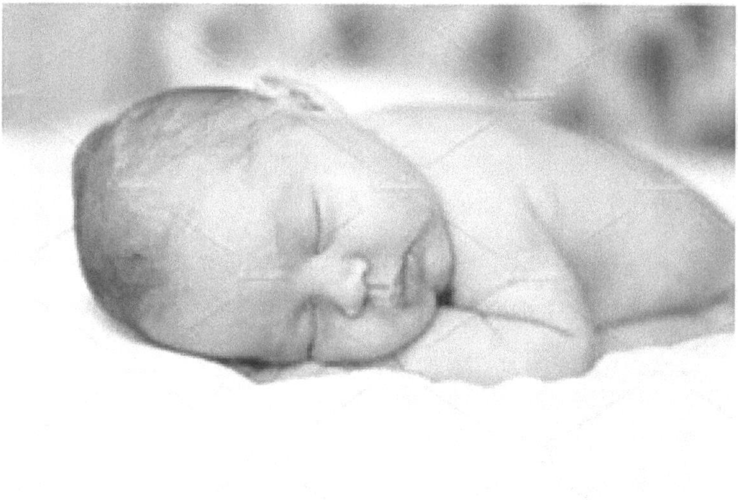

When Balanced:

1. Unconditional Love - The ability to give and receive love freely without judgment or attachment.
2. Compassion - Feeling empathy and understanding towards oneself and others.
3. Forgiveness - Letting go of past hurts and resentments, allowing for emotional healing.
4. Harmony - Creating and maintaining balanced relationships with others and oneself.
5. Connection - Feeling connected to others, nature, and the universe as a whole.
6. Emotional Balance - Experiencing emotions in a healthy and balanced way, without being overwhelmed by them.

7. Gratitude - Appreciating the beauty and abundance in life, feeling grateful for all experiences.
8. Acceptance - Accepting oneself and others as they are, without trying to change or control them.
9. Peace - Feeling an inner peace and tranquillity, even in the midst of challenges.
10. Self-Love - Having a deep sense of self-worth and self-acceptance, nurturing oneself with love and care.

When the Heart Chakra is balanced, these qualities are present in one's thoughts, feelings, and actions, leading to a sense of fulfilment, harmony, and connection in life.

Affirmations:

1. "I am worthy of love and compassion."
2. "I forgive myself and others, releasing all resentment and anger."
3. "My heart is open to giving and receiving love unconditionally."
4. "I am grateful for the abundance of love in my life."
5. "I am connected to the infinite power of love that flows through me."
6. "I am compassionate towards myself and others."
7. "I trust in the wisdom of my heart to guide me in all matters."
8. "I radiate love and kindness to all beings."

9. "I am at peace with myself and the world around me."

10. "My heart is filled with joy, harmony, and gratitude."

Repeat these affirmations regularly to open and balance your Heart Chakra, fostering love, compassion, and connection in your life.

CHAPTER 5

THROAT CHAKRA (VISHUDDHA)

The Throat Chakra, Vishuddha, is the fifth chakra located at the base of the throat. It governs communication, self-expression, and creativity. Represented by the colour blue and associated with the element of ether, it enables the clear, honest, and authentic expression of thoughts and emotions. A balanced Throat Chakra fosters effective communication with others and encourages listening attentively. Imbalances can lead to either excessive or deficient communication. Practices like meditation, chanting, and mindful communication can help balance the Throat Chakra, promoting clear expression, creativity, and harmonious interaction with others.

- Location - Throat
- Element - Sound
- Colour – Bright blue
- Sound - Ham
- Gland – Thyroid, parathyroid
- Crystal - Blue Lace Agate, Aquamarine, Lapis Lazuli, Turquoise, Sodalite

- Aroma – Peppermint, Eucalyptus, Lavender, Chamomile, Frankincense
- Produce a variety of hormones - adrenaline, steroids, aldosterone and cortisol
- Their functions include the regulation of metabolism and the immune system.
- Sense - Hearing
- Deals with Self-expression, chanting, vibration, communication, telepathy, creativity, ether

Characteristics of Throat Chakra:

It governs communication, self-expression, and creativity. Balanced Throat Chakra enables clear, honest, and authentic expression of thoughts, feelings, and ideas. Individuals with a healthy Throat Chakra communicate confidently, listening attentively and speaking truthfully. They express themselves creatively, embracing their unique talents and perspectives. Diplomatic and respectful communication is emphasised, fostering understanding and harmony in relationships.

An empowered Throat Chakra promotes confidence in one's ability to communicate effectively, advocating for oneself and others. It encourages active listening and receptivity, enabling individuals to understand and empathise with others' perspectives. Creativity flourishes as the Throat Chakra inspires artistic expression and innovation.

Imbalances in the Throat Chakra can manifest as either excessive or deficient communication. An overactive Throat Chakra may lead to talking excessively or speaking without consideration for others, while an underactive Throat Chakra can result in difficulty expressing oneself or feeling creatively blocked.

1. Gateway to Consciousness - Visual representations Telepathy - Finding silence within loud music
2. Media - For example, creating reels or posting ads on social media
3. Creativity - Confident in sharing their unique perspectives, leading to enhanced creative inspiration and innovation.
4. Resonance - Recognising patterns, like how long-term couples may start to resemble each other
5. Vibration - Observing the formation of shapes like mandalas or chakras in sand or powder placed on a vibrating music or sound system.

Practices such as meditation, chanting, and mindful communication can help balance the Throat Chakra, promoting clear expression, creativity, and harmonious interaction with others.

Self-Test:

Answer in Yes or No

1. Are you a good listener?
2. Are you organised?
3. Are you living a purposeful life?
4. Are you good at convincing others?
5. Are you good at communication?
6. Do you consider yourself a loyal person?
7. Do you like to write your thoughts and feelings, whether on social media or elsewhere?
8. Do you have a good ability to plan and organise?

If any of these or both are not aligned, then the person may have financial issues (linked to the Root Chakra).

9. Do you value truth and expect the same from others?

Results:

Check if your answer is Yes or No. If you get 'Yes' then see the results below;

8-9 – Excellent

5-7 – Good

2-4 – Can be better

0-1 – Best of luck

If Blocked:

When the Throat Chakra is blocked or imbalanced, it can manifest in various physical, emotional, and mental symptoms. Some common signs of a blocked or imbalanced Throat Chakra include:

1. Difficulty expressing oneself - Individuals may find it challenging to articulate their thoughts, feelings, or ideas. They may feel tongue-tied or have a sense of being unable to speak up.
2. Fear of public speaking - There may be a fear or anxiety surrounding speaking in public or expressing oneself in front of others.
3. Communication issues - There may be misunderstandings or conflicts in communication, both in personal and professional relationships. Individuals may struggle to communicate effectively, leading to frustration and resentment.
4. Creative blocks - A blocked Throat Chakra can inhibit creativity and self-expression. Individuals may feel uninspired or creatively stifled.
5. Sore throat or neck problems - Physical symptoms such as throat pain, frequent sore throats, neck stiffness, or thyroid issues may occur.
6. Dishonesty or manipulation - In some cases, individuals may resort to dishonesty or manipulation as a means of compensating for their inability to communicate authentically.

7. Feeling unheard or invalidated - Individuals with an imbalanced Throat Chakra may feel like their voice is not being heard or that their opinions and ideas are not being taken seriously.
8. Social withdrawal - There may be a tendency to withdraw from social interactions or avoid situations where communication is required.

Emotional Impacts:

When the Throat Chakra is blocked or imbalanced, emotional issues may arise, including difficulty expressing oneself, feeling unheard, fear of speaking up, frustration, inhibited creativity, social withdrawal, and sometimes, resorting to dishonesty or manipulation. These imbalances can lead to internal conflicts, strained relationships, and a lack of fulfilment. Individuals may experience anxiety, resentment, or a sense of disconnection from their authentic selves. Balancing the Throat Chakra through practices such as meditation, communication exercises, and creative expression can help alleviate these emotional issues and promote clarity, authenticity, and emotional well-being.

Balancing the Throat Chakra through practices such as meditation, chanting, journaling, and mindful communication can help alleviate these symptoms and promote clear, authentic self-expression.

Physical Impacts:

Physical impacts of a blocked Throat Chakra can manifest as various symptoms, including:

1. Throat pain or discomfort
2. Frequent sore throats or infections
3. Neck stiffness or tension
4. Thyroid gland issues
5. Difficulty speaking
6. Mouth ulcers or dental problems
7. Jaw pain or temporomandibular joint (TMJ) dysfunction
8. Earaches or ear infections

These physical symptoms may arise as a result of the energetic imbalance in the Throat Chakra and can often be linked to difficulties in communication, self-expression, or creative blockages. Addressing the underlying energetic imbalance through chakra balancing techniques, along with proper medical care, if necessary, can help alleviate these physical symptoms.

Relationship Impacts:

1. Communication issues - Difficulty expressing thoughts and emotions can lead to misunderstandings, conflicts, or lack of clarity in relationships.
2. Feeling unheard or invalidated - Partners may feel ignored or unappreciated if one or both individuals

struggle to communicate effectively.

3. Fear of speaking up - One partner may hesitate to express needs or desires, leading to unmet expectations or resentment.
4. Lack of intimacy - Inhibited communication can hinder emotional intimacy and vulnerability in relationships.
5. Disharmony - Unresolved conflicts or suppressed emotions can create tension and discord in the relationship.
6. Social isolation - A fear of judgment or rejection may lead to withdrawal from social interactions, impacting the couple's social life.
7. Trust issues - Difficulty being authentic or honest due to blocked communication channels can erode trust between partners.

If Over Energised:

When the Throat Chakra is over-energised, it can lead to various symptoms and issues, including:

1. Excessive Talking - Individuals may find themselves talking excessively, sometimes without considering the impact of their words on others.
2. Dominating Conversation - There may be a tendency to dominate conversations, interrupt others, or monopolise discussions.
3. Argumentative Behaviour - Over-energised Throat

Chakra can lead to a confrontational or argumentative communication style.

4. Harsh or Critical Speech - Individuals may speak harshly or critically, causing hurt feelings or damaging relationships.
5. Inability to Listen - There may be a lack of receptivity to others' perspectives or difficulty in truly listening to what others have to say.
6. Restlessness - Over-energised Throat Chakra can lead to feelings of restlessness or agitation.
7. Imbalance in Relationships - Excessive communication or dominance in conversations can create imbalances in relationships, leading to conflicts or misunderstandings.

Balancing activities such as meditation, mindful communication, and self-awareness practices can help bring the Throat Chakra back into equilibrium.

When Balanced:

When the Throat Chakra is balanced, individuals experience several positive outcomes:

1. Clear Communication - They can express themselves confidently and articulately, fostering healthy relationships and effective communication.
2. Authentic Expression - They communicate authentically, expressing their thoughts, feelings, and needs with honesty and integrity.

3. Creative Inspiration - Balanced Throat Chakra promotes creativity, allowing individuals to explore and express their unique talents and ideas.
4. Active Listening - They listen attentively to others, value different perspectives, and foster mutual understanding in relationships.
5. Harmonious Relationships - Clear communication and authenticity lead to harmonious relationships, free from misunderstandings or conflicts.
6. Emotional Expression - They feel comfortable expressing their emotions, leading to a greater sense of emotional well-being and fulfilment.
7. Self-Confidence - Balanced Throat Chakra instils confidence in one's ability to communicate effectively, contributing to overall self-assurance and empowerment.

Overall, a balanced Throat Chakra enhances communication, creativity, and authenticity, leading to improved relationships, emotional well-being, and personal growth.

Food:

Foods that are soothing and hydrating can help balance the Throat Chakra. Some preferred foods to balance the Throat Chakra include:

1. Herbal teas - Chamomile tea, peppermint tea, and

liquorice tea can help soothe the throat and promote clear communication.

2. Fruits - Particularly fruits with high water content, such as watermelon, oranges, and berries, can help keep the throat hydrated.
3. Soups and Broths - Warm soups and broths, especially those made with vegetables and herbs, can be comforting and nourishing for the Throat Chakra.
4. Coconut Water - Coconut water is hydrating and can help maintain moisture in the throat.
5. Honey - Raw honey is soothing for the throat and can be added to herbal teas or warm water.
6. Herbal Remedies - Herbs like slippery elm, marshmallow root, and sage have traditionally been used to soothe the throat and support vocal health.
7. Blue-Coloured Foods - Blueberries, blackberries, and other naturally blue-coloured foods can help stimulate the Throat Chakra.

Overall, choosing foods that are hydrating, soothing, and supportive of vocal health can help balance and nourish the Throat Chakra.

Yoga Poses:

Several yoga poses can help balance the Throat Chakra by opening and activating the neck and throat area. Some of the best yoga poses for balancing the Throat Chakra include:

1. Fish Pose (Matsyasana) - Opens the throat and chest, stimulating the Throat Chakra and promoting clear communication.

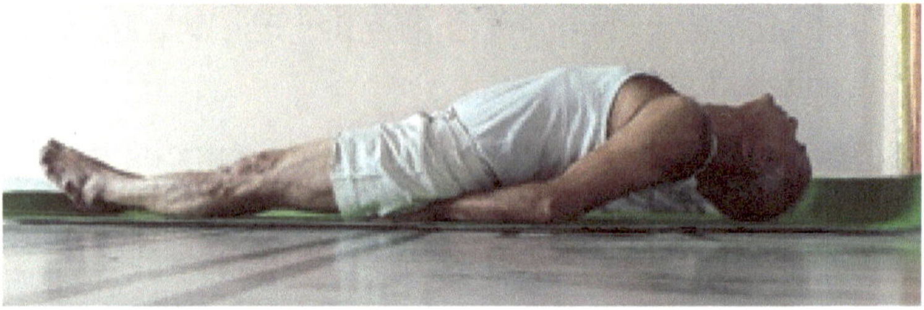

2. Bridge Pose (Sethu Bandhasana) - Stretches the neck and chest, helping to release tension and promote self-expression.

3. Camel Pose (Ustrasana) - Opens the throat and chest, stimulating the Throat Chakra and encouraging authenticity in communication.

4. Shoulder Stand (Sarvangasana) - Improves circulation to the throat and thyroid gland, promoting balance and vitality in the Throat Chakra.

5. Plow Pose (Halasana) - Stretches the neck and shoulders, helping to release tension and improve communication.

6. Lion's Breath (Simhasana) - A pranayama (breathing) exercise that helps release tension in the throat and promotes clear communication. To practice Lion's Breath in yoga, sit in a comfortable position, inhale deeply, then exhale forcefully while sticking out your tongue and roaring like a lion.

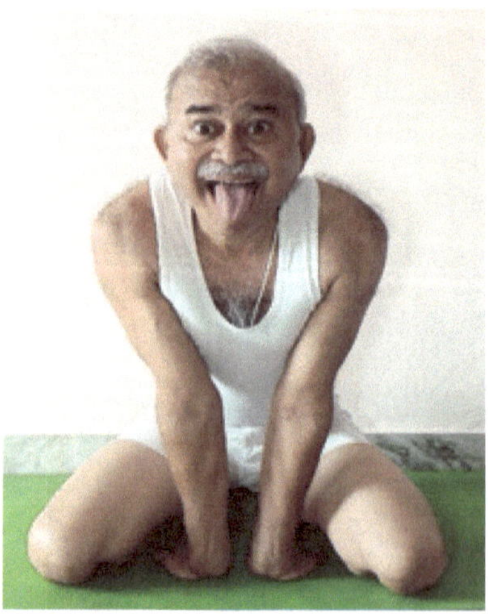

7. Supported Fish Pose (Matsyasana variation with props): Using props like a bolster or yoga blocks to support the back and head, allowing for a deeper opening of the throat and chest.

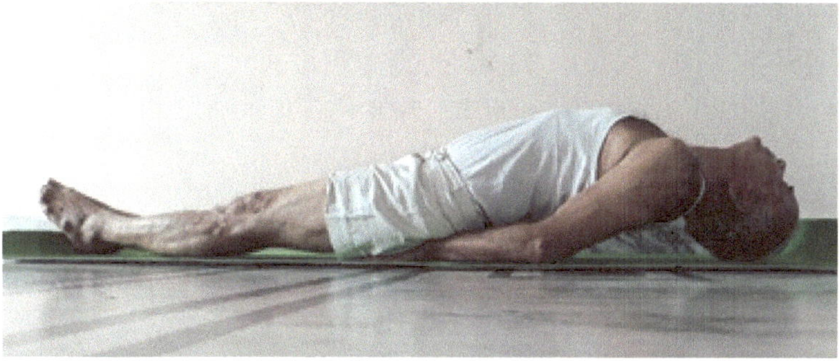

8. Cat-Cow Pose (Marjaryasana-Bitilasana): Alternating between arching and rounding the spine, this pose helps to release tension in the neck and throat while promoting flexibility and balance in the Throat Chakra.

Practising these yoga poses mindfully and with awareness of the breath can help balance and harmonise the Throat Chakra, promoting clear communication, self-expression, and authenticity.

Activity 1

- Rinse your mouth with water (Gargle)
- Speak with increased volume
- Perform energetic jumps, feeling vibrations up to your hips
- Let out a forceful scream from your abdomen
- Sing a song aloud
- Engage in journal writing
- Express yourself through poetry or book writing

Activity 2

Step 1: Inhale deeply.

Step 2: Close your nostrils.

Step 3: Bring your chin to your shoulder or chest.

Step 4: Swallow saliva three times, blocking your ears.

Step 5: Breathe normally.

Repeat this process three times.

Activity 3:

Sounds to Unblock:

- "OM" or "AUM" is akin to "AMEN", representing the original sound created by the Universe.
- "GATE GATE PARAGATE PARASAMGATE BODI SWAHA" is a Tibetan Smaller Heart Sutra.

- "I AM THAT I AM" uniting the individual with the universe.
- "OM NAMAH SHIVAYA"
- "I AM STRONG"
- "SO BE IT" - Tathaasthu

Affirmations:

Affirmations for balancing and aligning the Throat Chakra:

1. "I express myself with clarity and authenticity."
2. "My voice is powerful, and my words have value."
3. "I communicate confidently and effectively."
4. "I speak my truth with courage and integrity."
5. "I listen attentively and speak with compassion."
6. "Creativity flows freely through me."
7. "I embrace my unique talents and express myself creatively."
8. "I trust my intuition and communicate from the heart."
9. "I am open to receiving and expressing love and understanding."
10. "I honour my voice and speak the truth with confidence."

Healthy lifestyle:

Maintaining your physical body with proper nutrition requires a disciplined routine in life. Ensure a balanced diet rich in fruits, vegetables, lean proteins, and whole grains to provide essential nutrients. Hydration is crucial, so drink plenty of water throughout the day. Incorporate regular exercise to promote strength, flexibility, and cardiovascular health. Prioritise adequate sleep to support overall well-being and allow for proper recovery. Limit processed foods, sugar, and unhealthy fats, opting instead for wholesome, nutrient-dense options. Consistency is key, so commit to making healthy choices daily to nourish and support your body's needs. To alkalise your body and maintain pH levels:

1. Upon waking up in the morning, drink hot water, lemon water, or wheatgrass on an empty stomach.
2. Consume 5 soaked almonds and 2 walnuts.
3. Drink enough water during the day.
4. Take a 15–30-minute walk during sunrise and sunset, as well as after every meal.
5. For breakfast, include protein with your normal meal, such as 100-200g of sprouts.
6. Eat one fruit per day.
7. Have a salad before every meal to balance alkaline intake before consuming acidic foods.
8. In the evening, consume a detox soup made from blended vegetables.
9. Engage in daily exercise for at least 15-30 minutes at any time during the day.
10. Ensure quality sleep by going to bed between 10 pm and 2 am without disturbances.

Note: Eat fresh, living foods as much as possible. Incorporate fasting into your routine once a week.

CHAPTER 6

THIRD EYE CHAKRA (AJNA)

The Third Eye Chakra, known as Ajna in Sanskrit, is the sixth of the seven main chakras in the body. Located in the centre of the forehead, between the eyebrows, it is associated with intuition, perception, and inner wisdom. The Third Eye Chakra governs our ability to see beyond the physical realm and perceive the subtle energies of the universe.

When the Third Eye Chakra is balanced and open, individuals experience heightened intuition, clarity of thought, and a deep sense of connection to their inner guidance. They trust their instincts and have a keen awareness of the interconnectedness of all things. This chakra is also associated with imagination, visualisation, and psychic abilities.

Imbalances in the Third Eye Chakra can manifest as difficulties in decision-making, lack of clarity, or feeling disconnected from one's intuition. Physical symptoms may include headaches, vision problems, or sinus issues.

To balance and activate the Third Eye Chakra, individuals can practice meditation, visualisation, and mindfulness exercises. Spending time in nature, engaging in creative activities, and working with indigo-coloured crystals such as Amethyst or Lapis Lazuli can also help stimulate the energy of the Third Eye Chakra, promoting inner vision and spiritual awakening.

- Location – Between eyebrows, slightly above eye level
- Element - Light
- Colour - Indigo
- Sound - OM
- Gland – Pineal
- Crystal – Amethyst, Lapis Lazuli, Fluorite, Clear Quartz, Sodalite
- Aromas – Lavender, Frankincense, Sandalwood, Jasmine
- Deals with – Colour, seeing, intuition, visualisation, imagination, vision.

Characteristics of the Third Eye Chakra:

1. Intuition - The Third Eye Chakra is associated with intuition, insight, and inner wisdom. It enables individuals to trust their inner guidance and perceive beyond the physical realm.
2. Perception - This chakra governs perception, allowing individuals to see situations, people, and events with clarity and discernment.

3. Imagination - The Third Eye Chakra is linked to imagination and visualisation, enabling individuals to envision possibilities and manifest their desires.
4. Awareness - It fosters awareness of oneself and the world, leading to a deeper understanding of spiritual truths and universal interconnectedness.
5. Insight - The Third Eye Chakra facilitates deeper understanding and insight into life's mysteries, spiritual concepts, and the nature of existence.
6. Psychic Abilities - It is associated with psychic abilities such as clairvoyance, telepathy, and precognition, enabling individuals to access higher realms of consciousness.
7. Balance - A balanced Third Eye Chakra promotes mental clarity, intellectual growth, and emotional stability, fostering a harmonious connection between mind, body, and spirit.

Self-test:

Answer in Yes or No:

1. Are you creative?
2. Are you intuitive?
3. Do you listen to your inner voice?
4. Are you a keen observer?
5. Do you trust your intuition?
6. Are you connected with nature?

7. Do you enjoy learning new things?
8. Do you believe in universal energy?
9. Are you attuned to your gut feeling?
10. Do you possess a vivid imagination?
11. Do you act based on instinct?

Results:

8-11 - Excellent

5-7 – Good

2-4 - Can be better

0-1 – Best of luck

If Blocked:

When the Third Eye Chakra is blocked or imbalanced, it can manifest in various physical, emotional, and spiritual symptoms. Some common effects of a blocked Third Eye Chakra include:

1. Difficulty concentrating or making decisions.
2. Lack of clarity and insight.
3. Feeling disconnected from intuition or inner wisdom.
4. Headaches or migraines.
5. Vision problems or eye strain.
6. Insomnia or disturbed sleep patterns.
7. Lack of imagination or creativity.

8. Feeling stuck or unable to progress spiritually.
9. Scepticism or disbelief in spiritual matters.
10. Feeling disconnected from higher consciousness or spiritual guidance.
11. Unaware of psychic abilities
12. Unable to remember dreams

Emotional Impacts:

Emotional imbalances resulting from a blocked Third Eye Chakra can manifest in various ways, impacting one's mental and emotional well-being. Some common emotional imbalances associated with a blocked Third Eye Chakra include:

1. Confusion - Difficulty processing information and making sense of situations.
2. Lack of Clarity - Feeling uncertain about one's path or purpose in life.
3. Closed-Mindedness - Resisting new ideas or perspectives, being overly sceptical.
4. Anxiety - Feeling overwhelmed by uncertainty and the unknown.
5. Lack of Imagination - Struggling to envision possibilities or think creatively.
6. Emotional Numbness - Feeling disconnected from one's emotions or inner self.

7. Indecisiveness - Difficulty making choices or committing to decisions.
8. Disconnection from Intuition - Ignoring inner guidance or intuition, relying solely on logical reasoning.
9. Overthinking - Getting caught up in excessive analysis and mental chatter.
10. Feeling Spiritually Disconnected - Sense of separation from higher wisdom or spiritual guidance.

Addressing these emotional imbalances involves working to open and balance the Third Eye Chakra through practices such as meditation, visualisation, energy healing, and introspection.

Relationships Impacts:

An imbalanced Third Eye Chakra can affect relationships in various ways, potentially leading to conflicts, misunderstandings, or difficulties in forming deep connections. Some causes of relationship issues associated with a blocked or imbalanced Third Eye Chakra include:

1. Lack of Empathy - Difficulty in understanding or empathising with others' perspectives and feelings.
2. Communication Problems - Struggles in effectively expressing thoughts, ideas, or emotions.
3. Closed-Mindedness - Resistance to considering alternative viewpoints or new ideas, leading to conflicts.

4. Lack of Trust - Difficulty trusting one's intuition or the intentions of others.
5. Over-Reliance on Logic - Relying solely on rationality and logic, neglecting intuition and emotional intelligence.
6. Misinterpretation of Cues - Misreading social cues or signals leads to misunderstandings.
7. Indecisiveness - Difficulty making decisions or committing to choices, causing strain in relationships.
8. Inability to See Beyond the Surface - Focussing only on superficial aspects of relationships, overlooking deeper connections.
9. Overthinking - Excessive analysis and overthinking can create barriers to genuine connection and intimacy.
10. Disconnect from Spirituality - Lack of spiritual connection or alignment can impact the depth and meaning of relationships.

Addressing these issues involves working to balance the Third Eye Chakra through practices such as meditation, mindfulness, self-reflection, and seeking guidance from intuition. This can lead to greater clarity, empathy, and understanding in relationships.

Addressing and balancing the Third Eye Chakra through meditation, energy work, and other holistic practices can help alleviate these symptoms and restore harmony to the mind, body, and spirit.

Physical Impacts:

An imbalanced Third Eye Chakra can manifest physical symptoms due to its connection with various bodily functions and systems. Some causes of physical issues associated with a blocked or imbalanced Third Eye Chakra include:

1. Headaches and Migraines - The Third Eye Chakra is located in the forehead, and its imbalance can lead to tension headaches or migraines.
2. Eye Problems - Vision issues, eye strain, or sensitivity to light may occur when the Third Eye Chakra is imbalanced.
3. Sinus issues - Disruptions in the flow of energy through the Third Eye Chakra can contribute to sinus congestion or discomfort.
4. Sleep Disturbances - Imbalance in the Third Eye Chakra may disrupt sleep patterns, leading to insomnia or restless sleep.
5. Neurological Symptoms - Imbalanced energy in the Third Eye Chakra might affect neurological functions, resulting in dizziness, vertigo, or nerve-related symptoms.
6. Hormonal Imbalance - The Third Eye Chakra is associated with the Pituitary Gland, which regulates various hormones in the body. Imbalance in this chakra can affect hormonal levels and lead to related issues.

7. Immune System Dysfunction - Disrupted energy flow through the Third Eye Chakra may weaken the immune system, making the body more susceptible to infections or illnesses.
8. Digestive Issues - Imbalance in the Third Eye Chakra can impact the function of the autonomic nervous system, potentially leading to digestive problems such as indigestion or stomach discomfort.
9. Fatigue and Lethargy - Physical and mental fatigue may result from the body's efforts to compensate for imbalances in the Third Eye Chakra.
10. Overall discomfort - Aches, pains, or sensations of discomfort in the head, face, or neck region may occur when the Third Eye Chakra is imbalanced.

Addressing these physical symptoms involves restoring balance to the Third Eye Chakra through practices such as meditation, energy healing, yoga, and lifestyle adjustments. Seeking guidance from healthcare professionals can also help address any underlying medical conditions contributing to physical discomfort.

If Over Energised:

When the Third Eye Chakra is over-energised or excessively active, it can lead to various imbalances and challenges. Some effects of an overactive Third Eye Chakra include:

1. Excessive daydreaming - Overactivity in the Third Eye Chakra may cause individuals to spend excessive amounts of time lost in daydreams, fantasies, or imagination, making it difficult to stay grounded in the present moment.
2. Hallucinations or Illusions - Heightened sensitivity and perception associated with an overactive Third Eye Chakra can lead to experiencing hallucinations or seeing things that aren't objectively present.
3. Difficulty Concentrating - Excessive mental activity and preoccupation with inner visions or insights may make it challenging to focus attention on practical tasks or responsibilities.
4. Insomnia or Disrupted Sleep - Overstimulation of the Third Eye Chakra can lead to difficulty falling asleep, restless sleep, or vivid dreams that disrupt restfulness.
5. Anxiety or Paranoia - Heightened sensitivity to subtle energies and psychic impressions may lead to feelings of anxiety, paranoia, or overwhelm, especially when unable to discern between inner intuition and external stimuli.
6. Detachment from Reality - Overemphasis on spiritual or metaphysical experiences may result in a detachment from mundane reality, leading to difficulties in relating to others or engaging in everyday activities.

7. Excessive Intellectualisation - Individuals with an overactive Third Eye Chakra may rely excessively on intellect and intuition, potentially overlooking practical considerations or rational thought processes.
8. Over-reliance on Psychic Abilities - Heightened intuition and psychic awareness associated with an overactive Third Eye Chakra may lead individuals to rely too heavily on psychic insights or spiritual guidance, neglecting other aspects of life.
9. Sensory Overload - Increased sensitivity to light, sound, and energy may result in sensory overload or overwhelm, making it challenging to function effectively in stimulating environments.
10. Lack of Discernment - An overactive Third Eye Chakra may lead to difficulty discerning between genuine spiritual insights and imagination, fantasy, or wishful thinking.

Addressing an overactive Third Eye Chakra involves practices aimed at grounding excess energy, such as meditation, mindfulness, spending time in nature, and balancing activities that engage the physical senses. Additionally, setting healthy boundaries and seeking support from spiritual or psychological professionals can help manage the effects of an overstimulated Third Eye Chakra.

Food:

Foods that are considered beneficial for balancing the Third Eye Chakra are those that promote clarity of mind, enhance intuition, and support spiritual awareness. Some examples include:

1. Dark Leafy Greens - Spinach, kale, and other dark leafy greens are rich in antioxidants and nutrients that support brain health and cognitive function, which can enhance mental clarity and focus.
2. Berries - Blueberries, strawberries, and other berries are packed with antioxidants that help protect brain cells from oxidative stress, promoting cognitive function and mental clarity.
3. Omega-3 Fatty Acids - Foods rich in omega-3 fatty acids, such as salmon, walnuts, and flaxseeds, support brain health and may enhance cognitive function, intuition, and spiritual awareness.
4. Nuts and Seeds - Almonds, pumpkin seeds, and other nuts and seeds are rich in nutrients like magnesium and zinc, which support brain health and may enhance mental clarity and intuition.
5. Herbal Teas - Certain herbal teas, such as Chamomile, Peppermint, and Lavender, are known for their calming and soothing properties, which can help quiet the mind and enhance spiritual awareness during meditation or introspection.
6. Water - Staying hydrated is essential for overall

health and well-being, including brain function. Drinking plenty of water throughout the day helps maintain mental clarity and supports spiritual practices.

7. Foods rich in antioxidants - Antioxidant-rich foods, such as colourful fruits and vegetables, help protect brain cells from damage caused by free radicals, promoting cognitive function and mental clarity.
8. Spices - Certain spices, such as turmeric, ginger, and cinnamon, have anti-inflammatory properties and may support brain health, enhancing mental clarity and spiritual awareness.
9. Raw or Lightly Cooked Foods - Some people believe that consuming raw or lightly cooked foods, such as fruits, vegetables, and sprouts, can help enhance energy flow and promote spiritual awareness.
10. Foods that Resonate with You - Ultimately, the best foods for balancing the Third Eye Chakra are those that resonate with you personally and support your overall health and well-being. Listening to your body's intuitive wisdom can help guide you in choosing the right foods to nourish your mind, body, and spirit.

Activities:

Activity 1:

- Limit screen time.
- Visualise indigo light.
- Journaling - Write down your dreams, intuitive insights, and reflections on your spiritual journey to enhance your connection to your inner wisdom.
- Share your wisdom with others or on social media.
- Ensure quality sleep (from 10 pm to 2 am) by following good sleep hygiene practices and practising deep breathing with full concentration (both sitting and lying down).
- Take spontaneous trips to natural surroundings such as parks or gardens.
- Creative Expression - Engage in creative activities like painting, drawing, or writing poetry to tap into your imaginative and intuitive abilities.
- Intuitive Eating - Listen to your body's intuitive cues when it comes to food choices, focusing on nourishing foods that support your overall well-being.

Activity 2:

Lower your chin and gaze towards your feet while breathing deeply with your eyes open. (Can be done anytime)

Activity 3:

Assume the dog poses with your head touching the floor.

Activity 4:

Close your eyes and place your palms together while focusing on your breathing.

Activity 5:

Activity to balance the Third Eye Chakra by scanning all chakras with colours and focussing on the energy levels of each:

1. Find a quiet and comfortable space where you can sit or lie down comfortably.

2. Close your eyes and take a few deep breaths to centre yourself and relax your body.

3. Visualise a bright indigo light at the centre of your forehead, representing your Third Eye Chakra. Imagine this light expanding and filling your entire head with its vibrant energy.

4. Now, bring your awareness to each of your chakras, starting from the Root Chakra at the base of your spine. Visualise each chakra as a spinning wheel of energy, starting with the colour red for the Root Chakra.

5. As you move up through each chakra, visualise the corresponding colour associated with it:

- Sacral Chakra (below the navel) - Orange

- Solar Plexus Chakra (above the navel) - Yellow
- Heart Chakra (centre of the chest) - Green
- Throat Chakra (throat area) - Blue
- Third Eye Chakra (between the eyebrows) - Indigo
- Crown Chakra (top of the head) - Violet or white

6. Take a moment to observe the energy level of each chakra. Notice if there are any areas that feel blocked, stagnant, or overly active.
7. When you reach the Third Eye Chakra, focus on it for a few breaths. Visualise the indigo light becoming brighter and more radiant, indicating a balanced and harmonious energy flow.
8. If you notice any imbalances or blockages in the Third Eye Chakra or any other chakra, gently breathe into that area and imagine the blockage dissolving or the energy becoming more balanced.
9. Continue this practice for a few minutes, scanning through all your chakras and bringing awareness to each one.
10. When you're ready, take a few more deep breaths and slowly open your eyes. Take note of any insights or sensations you experienced during the practice.

This activity helps to align and balance the energy centres in your body, promoting overall harmony and well-being, with a specific focus on the Third Eye Chakra for intuition and inner wisdom.

When Balanced:

When the Third Eye Chakra is balanced, individuals experience a sense of empowerment, self-confidence, and inner strength. They feel motivated to pursue their goals with determination and have a clear sense of purpose in life. Emotionally, they exhibit a healthy level of self-esteem and assertiveness, allowing them to establish boundaries and make decisions confidently. Physically, they enjoy good digestion and metabolism, as well as a strong and resilient immune system. In relationships, they are able to assert themselves while also respecting the needs of others, fostering harmonious interactions. Overall, a balanced Third Eye Chakra enables individuals to navigate life challenges with resilience and optimism.

Affirmations:

1. "I trust my intuition and inner wisdom."
2. "I am open to receiving insights and guidance from the universe."
3. "My mind is clear, and my vision is focused."
4. "I trust the signals my body sends me."
5. "I see beyond the surface and perceive the deeper truths."
6. "I am connected to my higher self and divine

intelligence."

7. "I honour my inner knowing and act upon it with confidence."
8. "I am in tune with my inner guidance system."
9. "I am open to exploring new perspectives and ideas."
10. "I am the master of my thoughts, and I choose to see the world with clarity and insight.

Auras

Aura and its Alignments in Conjunction with Chakras

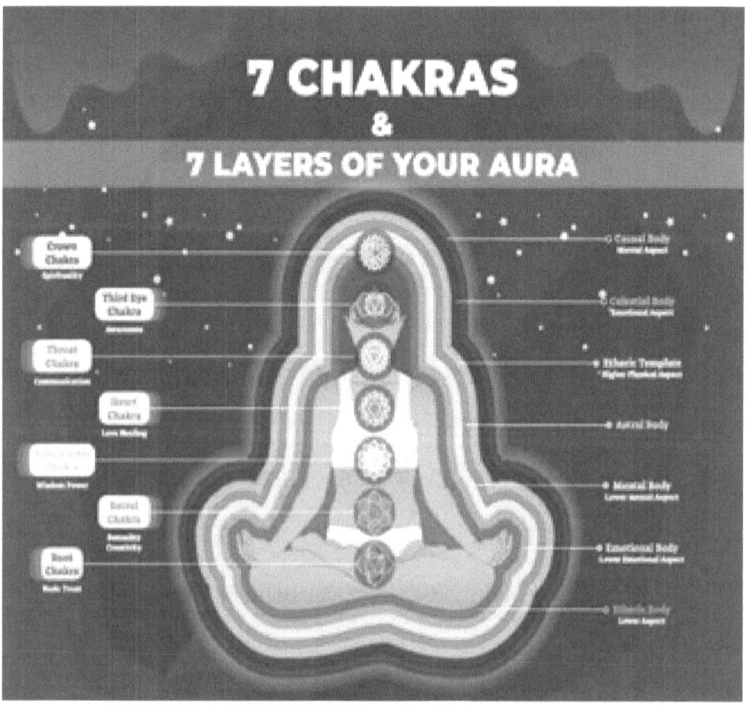

The aura, often described as the subtle energy field surrounding the human body, is intricately connected with the chakras, Ida, Pingala, and Sushumna energy pathways. Each layer of the aura corresponds to different aspects of the physical, emotional, mental, and spiritual self, and these layers interact with the chakras and energy pathways to maintain overall balance and well-being.

In various spiritual and energy healing traditions, it's believed that the human aura consists of multiple layers, each with its own unique qualities and functions. While the exact number and classification of aura layers may vary depending on the tradition or perspective, a commonly referenced model describes seven main layers of the aura. These layers are often described as follows:

1. Physical Aura - The Physical Aura is the closest layer to the physical body and is associated with physical sensations, vitality, and health. It reflects the physical condition of the individual and interacts closely with the physical body.
2. Etheric Aura - The Etheric Aura extends slightly beyond the physical body and is associated with life force energy or prana. It serves as the template for the physical body and is responsible for maintaining vitality and supporting physical functions. It is connected to the Root Chakra and has a light grey and blue colour.
3. Emotional Aura - The Emotional Aura surrounds the Etheric Aura and reflects the individual's emotional

state, feelings, and moods. It is sensitive to emotional energies and can fluctuate in response to emotional experiences. Connected to Sacral Chakra.

4. Mental Aura - The Mental Aura extends beyond the Emotional Aura and is associated with thoughts, beliefs, and mental processes. It reflects the quality of the individual's thoughts and mental clarity, as well as their ability to focus and concentrate. Connected to the Solar Plexus Chakra, its colour is yellow.
5. Astral Aura - The Astral Aura extends further beyond the Mental Aura and is associated with the astral plane, a dimension of consciousness beyond the physical realm. It reflects the individual's desires, dreams, and subconscious mind. This layer of aura corresponds to the Heart Chakra and the colour of this layer is pink.
6. Spiritual Aura - The Spiritual Aura surrounds the Astral Aura and is associated with higher states of consciousness, spirituality, and connection to the divine. It reflects the individual's spiritual essence, wisdom, and spiritual evolution. The celestial body corresponds to the Third Eye Chakra and the colour of this aura consists of multiple beams of bright, white light.
7. Casual Aura - The Divine Aura is the outermost layer of the aura and represents the individual's

connection to the divine or universal consciousness. It transcends individual identity and reflects the individual's oneness with all of creation. Casual body corresponds to your Crown Chakra and the colour of this aura consists of golden threads of light.

These seven layers of the aura are interconnected and interact with each other to create the overall energy field surrounding the individual. Balancing and harmonising these layers is essential for promoting health, well-being, and spiritual growth.

All these auras stem from the energy emanating from your 7 chakras. Each layer of your aura corresponds to a vibrational energy field linked to one chakra. The outer auric layers are larger and vibrate at higher frequencies. The size of your auric field is influenced by your physical, emotional, and spiritual well-being. When your chakras are balanced and you're feeling healthy, your aura can expand to several meters in radius, appearing light in colour. Conversely, your auric field may contract when your chakras are misaligned. While many intuitive individuals may perceive or see some of these auric fields, few can discern all seven layers.

I would like to share my experience with aura reading. I often experience clairvoyance and lucid dreaming, through which I have manifested my desires and received messages from others with whom I am connected.

One of the most exciting experiences occurred at the

QLU campus in Vikarabad, Telangana, during a program in December 2023. We had sessions on aura reading, Kundalini awakening, and chakra activation. During an exercise, I was paired with a stranger and tasked with reading their aura. I saw images, colours, and texts, mostly in black and white, as well as spiritual guides. To my surprise, my validations were 100% correct, which was acknowledged by the crowd of approximately 200 meditators.

After the session, my ability to see auras with open eyes persisted for about a month, and I even started reading auras from a distance and online. This experience inspired me to teach others to read auras independently, using techniques such as intuition and Ayurvedic Body Assessment.

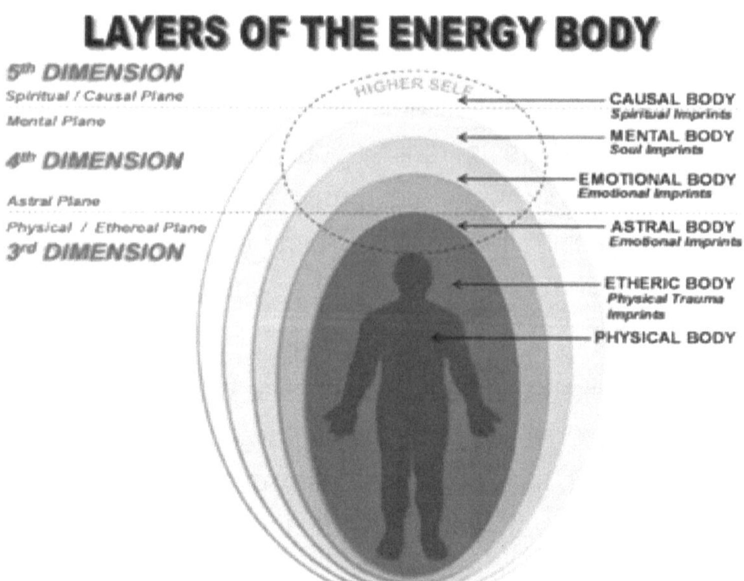

Many people spend thousands of dollars on readers to improve their health, but it's essential to recognise that the universe offers help in various forms, including messages from loved ones or signs in our surroundings. In this book, I explain how to read auras.

PS: I have included my own aura photo taken at the Meditators expo in March 2023, and my transformed photo on the cover page, taken in November 2023 after meeting the Akashic record master in July 2023.

For instance, spiritual masters such as the Dalai Lama and Sadguru - when they enter a city, accidents, illnesses among the people and the death rate tend to decrease. This phenomenon is attributed to their expansive auric fields, which vibrate at higher frequencies.

- The psyche influences the astral realm, which in turn affects the etheric plane and subsequently influences the physical body. Consequently, the mind wields control over the body.
- Persistently entertaining negative thoughts will impact the astral body, imbuing it with negativity, which then influences the etheric plane, rendering it dimmer and weaker over time, thus predisposing the physical body to illness.
- Maintaining good health requires avoiding constant fixation on stress, futile negative thoughts, and detrimental emotions.
- For instance, when individuals pass away or

experience accidents, they may still observe their lifeless bodies, witnessing medical professionals attending to them. This illustrates that they are not confined to their bodies, and neither are you.

- Choosing to consume more living foods like fruits and vegetables, focusing on uplifting aspects of life that inspire gratitude, and refraining from worrying about the unchangeable can significantly diminish the frequency of these occurrences.
- Nadis, Chakras & Aura - The Etheric field comprises three primary elements: nadis, chakras, and an aura. Many practitioners of yoga are familiar with the three primary nadis present within the physical body.

Aura Reading:

In aura reading, different colours are believed to correspond to different aspects of a person's physical, emotional, mental, and spiritual well-being. While interpretations can vary depending on the practitioner and tradition, here are some common colours and their general significance:

1. Red - Associated with vitality, strength, passion, and physical energy. A strong red aura may indicate a person who is energetic, passionate, and physically active, while a muddy or dark red aura may suggest anger, stress, or overstimulation.

2. Orange - Symbolises creativity, joy, enthusiasm, and emotional balance. An orange aura may indicate a person who is creative, sociable, and emotionally expressive, while a dull or muddy orange aura may suggest a need for emotional healing or creative blockages.
3. Yellow - Represents intellect, optimism, mental clarity, and confidence. A bright yellow aura may indicate a person who is intelligent, optimistic, and mentally focused, while a pale or murky yellow aura may suggest feelings of insecurity, mental fatigue, or lack of clarity.
4. Green - Signifies growth, balance, healing, and harmony. A vibrant green aura may indicate a person who is compassionate, nurturing, and emotionally balanced, while a dark or dull green aura may suggest jealousy, resentment, or unresolved emotional issues.
5. Blue - Associated with communication, intuition, truth, and spiritual awareness. A bright blue aura may indicate a person who is communicative, intuitive, and spiritually connected, while a cloudy or dark blue aura may suggest feelings of sadness, depression, or emotional repression.
6. Purple - Symbolises wisdom, spirituality, intuition, and higher consciousness. A deep purple aura may indicate a person who is spiritually evolved, intuitive, and connected to higher realms, while a

muddy or greyish purple aura may suggest psychic blockages or spiritual imbalance.

7. Pink - Represents love, compassion, and emotional healing. A pink aura may indicate a person who is loving, empathetic, and emotionally balanced, while a bright or vibrant pink aura may suggest feelings of romance or deep emotional connection.
8. White - Signifies purity, clarity, and spiritual enlightenment. A white aura may indicate a person who is spiritually evolved, pure of heart, and connected to higher dimensions, while a dull or murky white aura may suggest spiritual confusion or lack of clarity.

These interpretations are general guidelines, and individual experiences and perceptions may vary. It's essential to approach aura reading with an open mind and to consider the context and circumstances of each person's aura before making interpretations.

A standard aura imaging camera, which I acquired in February 2023, is used for providing psychic readings.

Each colour within the aura holds its own unique energy and significance, with distinct qualities and purposes. Visualise a colour wheel; every hue occupies a specific position on the wheel, with no colour deemed superior to another. Each colour imparts its inherent lessons, encompassing both positive and challenging traits.

In some interpretations of aura reading, the left side of the aura (from the viewer's perspective) is often associated with the past, while the right side is associated with the future. This perspective is based on the idea that the left side of the body is connected to the past, emotions, and subconscious mind, while the right side is connected to the future, action, and conscious mind.

On the left side of the aura photo (from the viewer's perspective): This signifies one's expressive, active, or masculine aspect—the persona projected outwardly and perceived by others. The colour in this area reflects the persona or how one presents oneself to the world. Additionally, it represents the recent past. The absence of colour or a void may denote a loss or a desire to release the past, such as through relocation or profound personal transformation.

On the right side of the aura photo (from the viewer's perspective), denotes one's feminine, receptive, or emotional facet—the part of the personality that receives, feels, accepts, and envisions. The colour here also reflects what one is manifesting for oneself in the near future. An abundance of colour suggests future-oriented focus, whereas a lack of colour may indicate dwelling on past memories.

At the centre of the aura photo, above the individual's head indicates the person's current experience. A band of colour arcing over the top of the photo signifies the individual's hopes, goals, and aspirations. For instance, an indigo or blue arc may symbolise spiritual or artistic aspirations, while a red arc could indicate monetary or business goals.

Expansive auras imply spiritual growth, expressiveness, extroversion, sociability, and a positive outlook, while closer auras suggest inward focus, sensitivity, and a desire for solitude, meditation, or tranquillity.

In aura reading, different colours are believed to correspond to different aspects of a person's physical, emotional, mental, and spiritual well-being. While interpretations can vary depending on the practitioner and tradition, here are some common colours and their general significance.

Activity:

Photographic Image or Blink:

Here's an activity to engage the Third Eye Chakra by using the blink-eye method to perceive the aura of another person:

1. Find a quiet and comfortable space where you and another person can sit facing each other.
2. Sit comfortably with your spine straight and relaxed, allowing for an open flow of energy.
3. Begin by closing your eyes and taking a few deep breaths to centre yourself and calm your mind.
4. With your eyes closed, focus your attention on the area between your eyebrows, where the Third Eye Chakra is located. Visualise a vibrant indigo light radiating from this point, illuminating your inner vision.
5. As you continue to breathe deeply, maintain your focus on the Third Eye Chakra, allowing the indigo light to expand and fill your entire head with its energy.
6. With your Third Eye Chakra activated, gently open your eyes and look at the other person without focusing directly on them. Instead, soften your gaze and allow your peripheral vision to come into play.
7. As you maintain this relaxed and receptive state, practice blinking your eyes slowly and intentionally. With each blink, remain open to the subtle energy field surrounding the other person.
8. Notice any shifts or changes in your perception as you blink your eyes. You may begin to sense or see colours, lights, or subtle movements in the space

around the other person.

9. Trust your intuition and inner guidance as you observe the other person's aura. Pay attention to any impressions or insights that arise during the practice.
10. After a few minutes of practising the blink-eye method, take a moment to reflect on your experience. Share your observations and insights with the other person if you feel comfortable doing so.

This activity helps to develop your intuitive abilities and expand your awareness of subtle energy fields, particularly the aura. By engaging the Third Eye Chakra and practising the blink-eye method, you can enhance your sensitivity to the energetic aspects of yourself and others.

Chakras Cleansing Process for Practitioners

To clean another person's chakras and provide energy, a practitioner typically uses techniques such as Reiki, Energy Healing, or Pranic Healing. Through intention and focused energy, the practitioner channels universal life force energy to the recipient, balancing and clearing their chakras. This may involve laying hands on or hovering over the body, visualising energy flow, and using symbols or mantras. The process can promote relaxation, release energetic blockages, and restore harmony to the recipient's energy system. However, it's essential to receive proper training and consent from the recipient before performing any energy-healing work.

Visit the AJ Life Mastery portal to learn how to assess other people's chakras, cleanse their aura, and offer blessings.

CHAPTER 7

CROWN CHAKRA (SAHASRARA)

The Crown Chakra, known as Sahasrara in Sanskrit, is the seventh primary chakra in the body's subtle energy system, according to Hindu and yogic traditions. Positioned at the top of the head, it represents the highest level of consciousness and spiritual connection. Sahasrara is associated with divine wisdom, enlightenment, and unity with the universe. It transcends individual identity and ego, allowing one to experience oneness with all creation. When the Crown Chakra is balanced and open, individuals may feel a deep sense of peace, bliss, and spiritual fulfilment. Practices such as meditation, prayer, and mindfulness can help activate and align the Crown Chakra, facilitating spiritual awakening and connection to higher realms of existence.

- Location – Top of the head
- Element - Thought
- Colour – Violet or white
- Mantra - "OM"
- Gland - Pituitary
- Crystals - Amethyst, Clear Quartz, Selenite,

5. Ametrine, Apophyllite

- Aromas – Sandalwood, Lavender, Rose, Lotus
- Food – None (fasting)
- Deals with – Consciousness, thought, information, knowing, understanding, transcendence, meditation and immense connection with the Divine.

Characteristics of the Crown Chakra:

The Crown Chakra, or Sahasrara in Sanskrit, possesses several characteristic traits and qualities:

1. Spiritual Connection - The Crown Chakra is the centre of spirituality and divine connection, symbolising unity with the universe and higher states of consciousness.
2. Enlightenment - It represents the pinnacle of spiritual growth and awakening, facilitating experiences of profound insight, wisdom, and enlightenment.
3. Oneness - The Crown Chakra transcends the ego and individual identity, fostering a sense of unity and interconnectedness with all of creation.
4. Divine Wisdom - This chakra governs access to divine knowledge and universal truths, allowing individuals to tap into higher levels of wisdom and understanding.
5. Inner Peace - A balanced Crown Chakra promotes a deep sense of inner peace, serenity, and contentment, regardless of external circumstances.

6. Connection to Higher Realms - It serves as a bridge between the physical and spiritual realms, facilitating communication with spiritual guides, angels, and higher beings.
7. Purpose and Meaning - The Crown Chakra helps individuals connect with their higher purpose and spiritual path, guiding them toward fulfilment and alignment with their soul's journey.
8. Transcendence - It represents transcendence beyond the limitations of the material world, encouraging individuals to seek spiritual growth and expansion of consciousness.
9. Awareness - A balanced Crown Chakra enhances awareness of the present moment and the interconnectedness of all existence, fostering a deep appreciation for the beauty and sacredness of life.
10. Bliss - Activation of the Crown Chakra can lead to experiences of profound bliss, ecstasy, and spiritual ecstasy as individuals align with the divine essence within themselves and the universe.

Overall, the Crown Chakra embodies the highest aspects of human consciousness and serves as a gateway to spiritual realisation and divine connection.

Self-test

1. Do you honour the divine within yourself?
2. Are you open to new ideas?

3. Do you feel worthy of divine love?
4. Are you able to let go of your attachments to the material world? For example, mobile phone usage: when, where, how much, and how to detach. (You can pinch yourself.) Attachment and detachment must be balanced.
5. Do you mostly live in the present in your thoughts?
6. Are you inspired by divine guidance?
7. Are you able to release doubt and welcome faith?
8. Are you aware of life and death? (Without guilt if you were to die in the next moment)
9. Are you aware of illusion and reality? (For example, closing your eyes during the daytime).
10. Are you aware of oneness?

Results:

8-10 Excellent

5-7 Good

2-4 Can be better

0-1 Best of luck

If Blocked:

When the Crown Chakra is blocked or imbalanced, it can manifest in various physical, emotional, and spiritual symptoms:

1. Feeling Disconnected - A blocked Crown Chakra may result in feelings of disconnection from the divine, a lack of spiritual fulfilment, or a sense of purposelessness.
2. Lack of Inspiration - Individuals with a blocked Crown Chakra may struggle to find inspiration or meaning in life, feeling uninspired and spiritually stagnant.
3. Closed-mindedness - There may be resistance to new ideas, spiritual beliefs, or experiences, leading to a closed-minded approach to life.
4. Depression or Anxiety - Imbalance in the Crown Chakra can contribute to feelings of depression, anxiety, or existential angst, as individuals grapple with questions of meaning and purpose.
5. Ego-Centric Behaviour - Instead of experiencing oneness and unity with all beings, there may be an overemphasis on the ego, leading to selfish or narcissistic behaviour.
6. Lack of Connection to Higher Self - A blocked Crown Chakra can hinder the connection to one's higher self, making it difficult to access intuition, inner wisdom, and spiritual guidance.
7. Physical Symptoms - Physical manifestations of a blocked Crown Chakra may include headaches, migraines, neurological issues, and disorders of the central nervous system.

8. Sleep Disturbances - Sleep disturbances such as insomnia or vivid dreams may occur when the Crown Chakra is blocked, reflecting inner turmoil and spiritual unrest.

To address a blocked Crown Chakra, individuals can explore various healing practices such as meditation, energy healing, yoga, mindfulness, and connecting with nature. Engaging in activities that promote spiritual growth and self-awareness can help restore balance to the Crown Chakra and foster a deeper connection to the divine and higher consciousness.

Emotional Impacts:

If the Crown Chakra is blocked, emotions can be profoundly impacted. Feelings of disconnection from the divine and others may lead to loneliness and spiritual emptiness. Depression, anxiety, and existential angst may intensify as individuals struggle to find meaning or purpose. Ego-centric behaviours may arise, diminishing empathy and fostering self-centredness. Fear, doubt, and scepticism about spiritual matters can increase, hindering faith and trust. Inspiration and motivation may wane, resulting in stagnation and creative blocks. Difficulty in letting go of attachments may perpetuate anxiety and insecurity. Healing practices can help open and balance the Crown Chakra, fostering emotional well-being and spiritual connection.

Relationship Impacts:

A blocked Crown Chakra can significantly impact relationships by hindering spiritual connection and empathy. Partners may feel emotionally distant, leading to feelings of loneliness or disconnection. Lack of trust in higher powers can cause scepticism or doubt, affecting faith in the relationship's purpose or direction. Ego-centric behaviours may emerge, diminishing empathy and understanding between partners. Difficulty in finding meaning or fulfilment can strain relationships as individuals grapple with existential questions. Healing the Crown Chakra can foster spiritual connection, empathy, and trust, enhancing the quality of relationships through deeper understanding, compassion, and alignment with a higher purpose.

Physical Impacts:

A blocked Crown Chakra can manifest physically in various ways. Headaches, migraines, and neurological issues may arise due to the chakra's location. Sleep disturbances, such as insomnia or vivid dreams, can occur as a reflection of inner turmoil and spiritual unrest. Disorders of the central nervous system may develop, affecting overall well-being. Chronic fatigue or lethargy may be present due to a lack of spiritual fulfilment. Physical symptoms can also include dizziness, vertigo, or light sensitivity. Balancing the Crown Chakra through healing practices like meditation and energy work can help alleviate these physical manifestations and promote overall health and vitality.

If Over Energised:

When the Crown Chakra is over-energised, it can lead to imbalances and challenges. Here are some potential effects:

1. Feeling Disconnected - Paradoxically, an overactive Crown Chakra can lead to feeling disconnected from the physical world or from others. There might be a preoccupation with spiritual matters to the extent of neglecting practical aspects of life or relationships.
2. Headaches and Migraines - Excessive energy in the Crown Chakra can manifest physically as headaches, migraines, or pressure sensations at the top of the head.
3. Spiritual Arrogance - An overactive Crown Chakra might lead to spiritual arrogance or superiority complex, where an individual believes they have exclusive access to divine knowledge or insights.
4. Difficulty Grounding - With excessive focus on spiritual matters, individuals may struggle with grounding themselves in the present moment or practical realities.
5. Feeling Overwhelmed - Too much energy in the Crown Chakra can overwhelm the individual,

leading to feelings of confusion, disorientation, or existential crisis.

6. Sleep Disturbances - Overstimulation of the Crown Chakra may disrupt sleep patterns, resulting in insomnia, vivid dreams, or other sleep disturbances.

To address an over-energised Crown Chakra, grounding practices such as spending time in nature, physical exercise, and mindfulness can help balance the energy flow and bring a sense of stability and harmony.

Yoga poses:

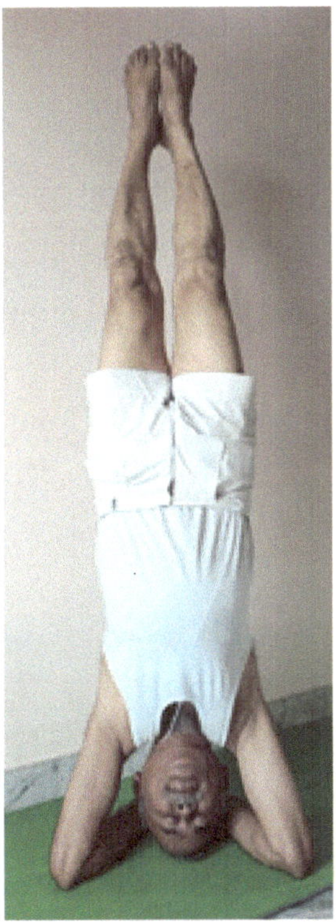

Yoga poses, also known as Asanas, can help balance the Crown Chakra by promoting relaxation, mindfulness, and energy flow throughout the body. Here are some yoga poses that can be beneficial for balancing the Crown Chakra:

1. Headstand (Sirsasana) -

Inversions like headstand increase blood flow to the brain, stimulating the Crown Chakra and promoting clarity of thought.

2. Lotus Pose (Padmasana) - Sitting in lotus pose can help create a sense of groundedness and stability while also opening up the energy channels in the body, including the Crown Chakra.

3. Supported Shoulder stand (Salamba Sarvangasana) - Similar to a headstand, a shoulder stand stimulates the Crown Chakra by increasing blood flow to the brain and promoting mental clarity.

4. Seated Meditation(Padmasana) - Simply sitting in a comfortable position and meditating can be highly effective for balancing the Crown Chakra. Focus on breathing deeply and visualising a bright white or violet light at the crown of the head.

5. Tree Pose (Vrksasana) -

This balancing pose promotes stability and inner strength while also encouraging a sense of connection to the higher self.

6. Child's Pose (Balasana) - This gentle forward bend helps to release tension and promote relaxation, allowing energy t0 flow freely throughout the body, including the Crown Chakra.

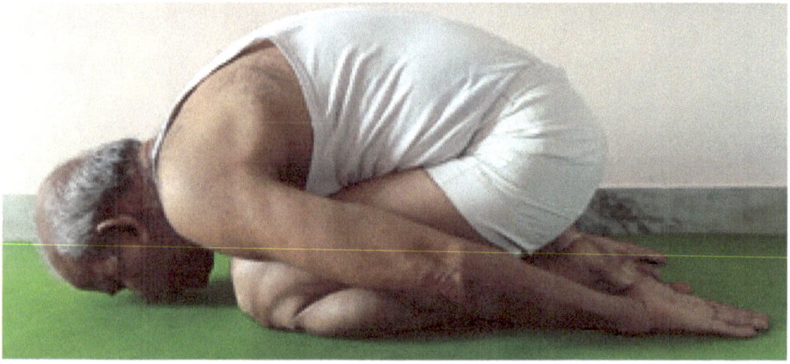

7. Corpse Pose (Savasana) - Finally, ending your practice with the corpse pose allows for deep relaxation and integration of the benefits of your practice, including balancing the Crown Chakra.

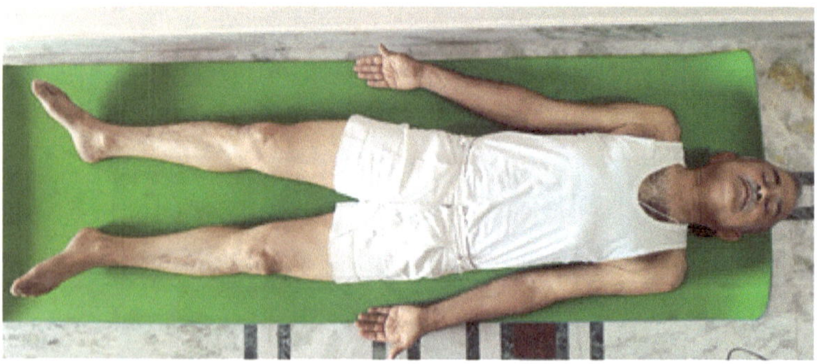

These yoga poses, when practised mindfully and with intention, can help to balance and harmonise the Crown Chakra, promoting spiritual connection, clarity, and enlightenment.

When Balanced:

When the Crown Chakra is balanced, individuals may experience a range of positive effects across physical, emotional, mental, and spiritual aspects of their lives:

1. Spiritual Connection - A balanced Crown Chakra fosters a deep sense of connection to the divine and higher consciousness, leading to feelings of unity, oneness, and spiritual fulfilment.
2. Clarity of Thought - Balanced energy in the Crown Chakra promotes mental clarity, insight, and intuition, allowing individuals to perceive higher truths and understand the interconnectedness of all things.
3. Inner Peace - With a balanced Crown Chakra, individuals experience a profound sense of inner peace, serenity, and contentment, regardless of external circumstances.
4. Spiritual Growth - The balanced flow of energy through the Crown Chakra supports spiritual growth and evolution, facilitating experiences of spiritual awakening, enlightenment, and expanded awareness.
5. Alignment with Higher Purpose - Individuals with a balanced Crown Chakra feel aligned with their higher purpose and soul's journey, guiding them towards fulfilling their spiritual mission and expressing their authentic selves.

6. Inspiration and Creativity - Balanced energy in the Crown Chakra enhances creativity, inspiration, and visionary thinking, allowing individuals to tap into their creative potential and manifest their dreams into reality.
7. Openness to Universal Wisdom - A balanced Crown Chakra fosters openness to receiving universal wisdom and guidance, enabling individuals to trust their intuition and follow the guidance of their higher selves.
8. Harmonious Relationships - Balanced energy in the Crown Chakra supports harmonious relationships based on mutual respect, compassion, and understanding, as individuals recognise the divine essence in themselves and others.

Overall, a balanced Crown Chakra leads to a state of higher consciousness, spiritual harmony, and holistic well-being, allowing individuals to live authentically and in alignment with their highest truth and purpose.

Activities:

Outer cleaning:

Outer cleansing for the Crown Chakra involves practices that help release stagnant energy and promote balance and harmony in your external environment. Here are some methods to cleanse the outer aspects of your Crown Chakra:

1. Smudging - Burn sacred herbs such as sage, Palo Santo, or cedarwood and allow the smoke to waft around your space. Visualise the smoke clearing away any negative or stagnant energy from your surroundings, including your Crown Chakra.
2. Sound Healing - Use sound vibrations to cleanse your environment. You can play Tibetan singing bowls, bells, or chanting to fill your space with positive vibrations that resonate with the Crown Chakra.
3. Crystals - Place crystals associated with the Crown Chakra, such as Clear Quartz, Amethyst, or Selenite, in your living or workspace. These crystals can absorb and transmute negative energy, promoting a harmonious environment.
4. Natural Light - Open windows and let natural sunlight into your space. Sunlight is a powerful cleanser and energiser, helping to uplift and purify the energy in your environment.
5. Decluttering - Clearing physical clutter from your space can also help declutter your mind and promote clarity of thought, which is beneficial for balancing the Crown Chakra. Remove any unnecessary items and organise your space to create a sense of openness and flow.
6. Energy Clearing Rituals - Perform energy-clearing rituals, such as visualisations or prayers, to release any negative or stagnant energy from

your surroundings. Use your intention and focus to direct positive energy towards balancing and harmonising your Crown Chakra and your environment.

By incorporating these practices into your routine, you can effectively cleanse the outer aspects of your Crown Chakra and create a supportive environment for spiritual growth and well-being.

Inner Cleaning:

Inner cleansing for the Crown Chakra involves practices that help release blockages and promote balance and harmony within your own energy system. Here are some methods to cleanse the inner aspects of your Crown Chakra:

1. Meditation - Practise Crown Chakra meditation to focus your attention on the energy centre at the top of your head. Visualise a bright white or violet light radiating from your Crown Chakra, cleansing and purifying it of any negative or stagnant energy.
2. Breathwork - Engage in deep breathing exercises to oxygenate your body and clear your mind. Focus on inhaling positive energy and exhaling any tension or negativity that may be blocking your Crown Chakra.
3. Affirmations - Repeat affirmations that are specifically tailored to balance and cleanse

the Crown Chakra. Affirmations such as "I am connected to divine wisdom" or "I trust in the guidance of the universe" can help align your energy with the qualities of the Crown Chakra.

4. Visualisation - Use the power of visualisation to imagine a stream of cleansing energy flowing through your Crown Chakra, washing away any impurities or blockages. Picture the energy centre becoming clear, vibrant, and open to receiving divine guidance and inspiration.
5. Energy Healing - Seek out energy healing modalities such as Reiki, acupuncture, or Pranic healing to balance and cleanse your Crown Chakra. These techniques can help remove energetic blockages and promote the free flow of energy throughout your body.
6. Journaling - Reflect on any thoughts, beliefs, or emotions that may be blocking your Crown Chakra. Write them down in a journal and explore ways to release and let go of anything that no longer serves your highest good.
7. Nature Connection - Spend time in nature to recharge and cleanse your energy. Connect with the natural world around you and allow the healing energy of Mother Earth to support your inner cleansing process.

By incorporating these practices into your routine, you can effectively cleanse and balance the inner aspects of your Crown Chakra, promoting spiritual growth, clarity, and connection to higher consciousness.

Other activities – Sit in silence, chant, practice deep breathing, and be with nature.

Consciousness Meditation

Here's how Consciousness Meditation can help you focus on observing thoughts for the Crown Chakra:

1. Preparation - Find a quiet and comfortable space to sit or lie down. Close your eyes and take a few deep breaths to centre yourself.
2. Set Your Intention - Set your intention to observe your thoughts without judgment or attachment. Remind yourself that you are simply an observer of your thoughts, not defined by them.
3. Focus on the Breath - Begin by bringing your awareness to your breath. Notice the sensation of the breath as it enters and exits your body. Allow your breath to become slow, deep, and rhythmic.
4. Observer Mode - Shift your focus to observing your thoughts as they arise. Imagine yourself sitting on the bank of a river, watching as thoughts flow by like leaves floating on the water. Whenever you notice a thought, simply acknowledge it and let it pass without getting caught up in its content.
5. Non-Attachment - Practice non-attachment to

your thoughts. Rather than engaging with them or trying to push them away, simply allow them to come and go on their own. Notice any emotions or reactions that arise, but avoid becoming entangled in them.

6. Return to the Breath - If you find yourself becoming distracted by thoughts or emotions, gently bring your focus back to the breath. Use the breath as an anchor to ground yourself in the present moment.
7. Expanded Awareness - As you continue to observe your thoughts, begin to expand your awareness beyond the individual thoughts themselves. Notice the space between thoughts, the underlying stillness that exists beneath the surface noise of the mind.
8. Crown Chakra Connection - Visualise a bright white or violet light emanating from the top of your head, symbolising the energy of the Crown Chakra. Imagine this light enveloping your entire being, filling you with a sense of clarity, wisdom, and spiritual connection.
9. Silent Witness - Rest in the state of silent witnessing, allowing yourself to simply be present with whatever arises in your awareness. Embrace a sense of spaciousness and expansiveness, knowing that you are the silent observer of your own inner world.
10. Closing - When you're ready to conclude the

meditation, take a few deep breaths and slowly bring your awareness back to your body and the present moment. Open your eyes and take a moment to reflect on your experience.

Practice of this consciousness meditation regularly can help you develop greater self-awareness, clarity of mind, and a deeper connection to the wisdom of your Crown Chakra.

Revealing the Secrets of the Akashic Records

The Akashic Records, according to certain spiritual beliefs and metaphysical teachings, are a compendium of all human events, thoughts, words, emotions, and intentions that have ever occurred in the past, present, or future. The term "Akashic" is derived from the Sanskrit word "Akasha," which means ether or space.

In essence, the Akashic Records are considered to be a kind of cosmic library or database that stores the collective wisdom and experiences of all souls. It is believed that every individual has their own unique "book" within the Akashic Records, containing information about their soul's journey across lifetimes.

Accessing the Akashic Records is often described as entering a state of deep meditation or altered consciousness, where individuals can tap into the universal consciousness to gain insights, guidance, and understanding about their life purpose, relationships, challenges, and potential future paths.

Practitioners who work with the Akashic Records may use various techniques such as meditation, visualisation, or guided imagery to access this realm and seek guidance from the higher realms of consciousness. It is considered a sacred and profound practice that can offer profound spiritual insights and healing.

I would like to share my experience accessing the Akashic Records and how I manifested my desires, particularly in pursuing a career in real estate and building construction.

During the pandemic, I lost my IT job and spent a year working with a construction company to learn the trade. Unfortunately, the company shut down due to the global economic crisis, leaving me without enough capital to start my own business. I was worried about mobilising funds and attracting clients, investors, and support in the industry.

I met a spiritual master in Melbourne at a meditation expo who practised hypnotherapy and could access the Akashic Records. In a two-hour session, I visualised images of places I had never seen before, including igloo houses and a vast library with golden walls and roofs. Through affirmations and prayers, she helped me remove blockages and attract opportunities in my desired fields globally.

With daily prayers and meditation, I witnessed remarkable improvements in my health, relationships, and finances. I connected with the right people, signed building contracts, and even started AJ Life Mastery, engaging in government projects.

Now, I want to share my knowledge and experiences to help others achieve their dreams. Through guided meditations and prayers, I aim to empower individuals to access the Akashic Records and manifest their desires.

How to Access Akashic Records:

Accessing the Akashic Records involves entering a deep meditative state or altered state of consciousness to connect with the universal consciousness. Here are steps commonly used by practitioners to access the Akashic Records:

1. Prepare for Meditation - Find a quiet and comfortable space where you won't be disturbed. Sit or lie down in a relaxed position.
2. Set Intentions - Set your intention to access the Akashic Records with respect, reverence, and openness to receiving guidance and insights.

3. Invoke Protection - Call upon your spiritual guides, angels, or higher self to protect and guide you during the process.
4. Enter a Meditative State - Begin by focussing on your breath, allowing your body and mind to relax. Release any tension or distractions.
5. Visualise a Sacred Space - Imagine yourself surrounded by a protective sphere of light. Visualise a sacred space such as a library or temple where the Akashic Records are stored.
6. Request Access - Mentally or verbally ask permission to access the Akashic Records. State your intention clearly and respectfully.
7. Receive Guidance - Pay attention to any images, sensations, thoughts, or insights that come to you. Trust your intuition and allow information to flow without judgment.
8. Ask Questions - If you have specific questions or areas of your life you'd like guidance on, ask them in a clear and concise manner. Be open to receiving answers in various forms.
9. Record Insights - After the session, take time to journal or record any insights, messages, or guidance you received from the Akashic Records.
10. Express Gratitude - Thank your spiritual guides, angels, or higher self for their assistance and guidance. Express gratitude for the insights received.

Remember that accessing the Akashic Records is a sacred and personal practice, and it may take time and practice to develop the ability to do so effectively. Trust your intuition and allow the process to unfold naturally.

On a daily basis, recite this Akashic Records prayer. Pray continuously for 21 days for enhanced results.

Opening prayer – Can be performed in the morning:

1. "So, we acknowledge the forces of Light, asking for courage, guidance, and direction to know the truth, as it is revealed for our highest good and for the good of everyone connected to us."
2. "Oh, Holy Spirit of God, protect me from all forms of self-centredness, and direct my attention to the work at hand."
3. "Help me know myself in the eyes of the Akashic Records, to see myself in the eyes of the Lords of the Records, and enable me to share the wisdom and compassion that the masters, teachers, and loved ones have for me."

Repeat part 3 once more. Then say, "The Records are now open."

Closing Prayer – Can be Performed Before going to Bed:

- "I express gratitude to the masters, teachers, and loved ones for their compassion and love."
- "I express gratitude to the Lords of the Records for their perspective."
- "I express gratitude to the Holy Spirit of Light for knowledge, wisdom, and healing."
- "The records are now closed. The records are now closed. The records are now closed."

Advantages of Meditation and Aligning Chakras:

Regular meditation and balancing chakras can make life smoother. Handle day-to-day life. You understand another person's situation and deal accordingly. You develop forgiveness and a giving nature. Surrender to the universe and observe what it has to offer you.

You may even develop ESP, like I have. I can see signs, images, patterns, text, and colours.

Recently, I gave readings to a few people where I could see their houses, family members, town landmarks, and who they're connected to. I could even predict past and future events and offer solutions to their problems when asked questions.

ESP, or extrasensory perception, refers to the purported ability to acquire information through means other than the known human senses (sight, hearing, touch, taste, and smell). This phenomenon encompasses various psychic abilities such as telepathy, clairvoyance, precognition, and psychokinesis.

1. Telepathy - The ability to perceive thoughts, emotions, or information from another person's mind without the use of known sensory channels.
2. Clairvoyance - The ability to perceive information about objects, people, events, or locations from a distance beyond the reach of the ordinary senses.
3. Precognition - The ability to perceive or predict future events before they occur, often through dreams, visions, or intuitive insights.

4. Psychokinesis - The ability to influence or manipulate objects, matter, or energy with the power of the mind alone, without physical interaction.

ESP phenomena have been the subject of much interest, research, and debate within various fields, including psychology, parapsychology, and neuroscience. While some individuals claim to have experienced or demonstrated ESP abilities, scientific evidence for the existence of such phenomena remains inconclusive, and sceptics often attribute reported experiences to coincidence, suggestion, or cognitive biases.

Despite the lack of empirical evidence, belief in ESP phenomena persists in many cultures and spiritual traditions, and research into the nature of consciousness and human potential continues to explore the boundaries of human perception and experience.

Lifestyle vision chart – Diet and exercise plans

I recommend readers make a vision board for their lifestyle. Look for sample goal charts for a healthy diet and fitness program. You can change your lifestyle with simple changes at home.

Exercise – Integrate into your daily routine:

Body movements are crucial for maintaining energy and balancing chakras. You can incorporate the following exercises into your schedule over the course of seven days, mixing and matching as desired.

- Take a 15–30-minute morning walk.
- After each meal, take a 30-minute break and walk for another 15-30 minutes.
- Aim for a total of 10,000 steps per day.
- For energy, engage in 30-45 minutes of weight training at the gym.
- To build stamina, participate in intense bodyweight exercises like Zumba for at least 30 minutes.

- Incorporate stretching by practicing yoga for 30-45 minutes.
- Include breathing exercises such as Anulom Vilom Pranayama.

You can do exercises any time during the day. It's best to do them in the morning because they give you energy and help with metabolism

DAYS	TIME	DURATION		
SUN	Morning 7am and Evening 5pm	15 mins-30mins	Breathing exercises(Pranayama) and Chakra Exercise	3 type x 5 rounds each
MON	Morning 7am and Evening 5pm	15 mins-30mins	Breathing exercises(Pranayama) and Yoga	Cleansing of chakras Each repeats for 2 times
TUES	Morning 7am and Evening 5pm	15 mins-30mins	Breathing exercises(Pranayama) and Body Resistance Training Or Weight Training-Gym	Weekly 2-3 times
WED	Morning 7am and Evening 5pm	15 mins-30mins	Breathing exercises(Pranayama) and Chakras Exercise	3 type x 5 rounds each
THURS	Morning 7am and Evening 5pm	15 mins-30mins	Breathing exercises(Pranayama) and Yoga (3 to 8 from above)	Cleansing of chakras Each repeats for 2 times
FRI	Morning 7am and Evening 5pm	15 mins-30mins	Breathing exercises(Pranayama) and Body Resistance Training	Weekly 2-3 times
SAT	Morning 7am and Evening 5pm	15 mins-30mins	Breathing exercises(Pranayama) and Body Resistance Training Or Weight Training-Gym	Weekly 2-3 times

Sample chart of a typical Indian diet plan: This plan includes balanced meals with protiens, carbs, and healthy fats.

DAY	PRE-BREKKIE	BREAKFAST	SALAD	LUNCH	SALAD	DINNER
SUN	Lemon water, fruit, almonds/walnut .	Millet dosa paneer or sprouts or tofu	Any combo	Brown rice veggies*2	Any combo	Detox soup brown or white rice veggies.
MON	Lemon water, fruit, almonds/walnut .	Veg dosa sprouts or omelet	Any combo	Brown rice dal, veggies*2	Any combo	Detox soup roti channa veg.
TUES	Lemon water, fruit, almonds/walnut .	Idli -millet sprouts	Any combo	Roti channa veg rice roti rajma veg	Any combo	Detox soup roti rajma and veg.
WED	Lemon water, fruit, almonds/walnut .	Idli or dosa or uttapam(millets) sprouts or panner	Any combo	Rice/ roti rajma veg	Any combo	Detox soup roti /rice dal, veg.
THURS	Lemon water, fruit, almonds/walnut .	Vegetable dosa sprouts or tofu	Any combo	Rice/ roti dal rajma veg	Any combo	Detox soup roti /rice channa, veg.
FRI	Lemon water, fruit, almonds/walnut .	Pooha with lots of sprouts.	Any combo	Rice/ roti channa veg	Any combo	Detox soup roti /rice channa, veg.
SAT	Lemon water, fruit, almonds/walnut .	Uttapam/ pesarattu speouts or tofu salad	Any combo	Rice/ roti veggies*2	Any combo	Detox soup roti /rice veggies.

PRE-BREKKIE	BREAKFAST	SALAD	LUNCH	SALAD	DINNER
Overnight soaked fenugreek seeds Citric fruit (Kiwi/orange/ pear/cherries / berries) Over night soaked 2x walnuts and 5x almonds	First have 1 bowl sprouts then,omlet/ indian pancake lentil pancake vegetable pancake , savory lentil pancake, flattened rice with lots of sprouts / lentil pancake/ mixed lentils steamed rice cakes,rice crepes	1x Bowl of salad. Raw / steam/ boiled / sauteed Combo of any cucumber, carrot, tomato, onion, boiled egg, capsicum, corn, lettuce, brocilli	Brown rice + lots of veggies + cottage cheese/boile / kidney beans/chickpe aschickpea, curry,lentil stew / protein source	1x Bowl of salad. Raw / steam/ boiled / sauteed Combo of any cucumber , carrot, tomato, onion, boiled egg, capsicum, corn, lettuce, brocilli	Detox soup Millet roti Sorghum, Finger millet Corn or Maize, Amaranth Indian cottage cheese , protien source.

Grains	Millets, brown rice , quinoa, oats, barley ,bread/ roti Sorghum, Finger millet, Corn or Maize, Amaranth
Protein's	Indian cottage cheese, boiled kidney beans, chickpeas, chickpea curry,lentil stew, chicken,salmon fish (protien source), pulses, soya , spinach
Vegetables	Cooked or roasted Avoid fried veggies ex: potatoes

MAGIC PLATE FOR BREAKFAST
5 Soaked Almonds
+ 1/2 Soaked Walnuts
OR

MAGIC PLATE FOR LUNCH
25%
Salad
25%
Protein (Lentils, Pulses, Sprouts, Paneer, Eggs)
Cooked Veggies/ Seasonal Vegetable Sabji
25%
Whole Grain (Jowar, Jau, Ragi, Makka, Rajgeera, Rice)
25%

MAGIC PLATE FOR DINNER
1/3
Soup
1/3
Steam or
Sautéed
Veggies
1/3
Carbs + Protein
Khichdi / Dal Rice /
Dal Chilla / Idli / Dosa

Gratitude and Giving:

Gratitude:

Show appreciation to the universe, people, and circumstances that have influenced your journey. Gratitude holds the potential to change your life and uncover unforeseen possibilities. Gratitude can take many forms, such as being thankful for being alive, healthy, and receiving love from family and friends. During challenging times or when results disappoint, remember the resilience of a tree - despite being battered by the wind, it breaks and rebuilds itself slowly.

I'd like to share an experience where I faced adversity within a community but managed to overcome it.

Several years ago, I was actively involved in a community organisation, playing a significant role. However, due to differences in opinion, I was compelled to depart from the organisation.

Initially, I felt disheartened as I had dedicated myself to serving the community with good intentions, going above and beyond my duties. Nevertheless, I later established my own not-for-profit organisation and received recognition, admiration, love, awards, rewards, and opportunities like never before. I always express gratitude to the previous organisation and the individuals who enabled me to move on and grow.

My gratitude goes to Sneh Desai for his programme 'Change Your Life'. It taught me how to harness the power of the universe and manifest my desires.

Giving:

I really believe in the power of giving. It changes your feelings from not having enough to having more than enough. You don't always have to give money. You can give your time, advice, help, suggestions, or even just a good idea that might make a difference in someone's life or make them feel better. Sometimes, the best gift is when you do it without anyone asking, like holding the door open for someone or letting people cross the road when you're driving. The universe notices these things.

I'd like to tell you about a couple of small incidents where I helped others. I was in India in April during the summer. It was midnight, and I was going home from the airport. There was a strike because taxi drivers weren't getting paid extra for using the air conditioner, as it uses more fuel. I asked the driver to roll down the windows and turn off the Air Condition. I also gave him an extra tip because he got me home safely. On the way, I offered him a complimentary meal plan because he was experiencing some health issues.

I want to share some advice I gave to a friend that helped them feel better. My friend had a disagreement with someone, and it bothered them whenever they saw or thought about that person. Imagine you're driving your car, and you see a mentally challenged person throwing stones at it. In such a situation, we understand that they're not mentally well, so we decide to ignore them and just keep driving. If things get worse, they can take action by reporting to someone, or you can get away from them and forgive them for what they did. It might seem like simple advice, but it can really help when you're feeling overwhelmed. The best thing to do is forgive and move on. I believe the universe sees what you do and gives back to you what you give to others. It's called the law of karma.

SMART goals:

S stands for Specific.

M stands for Measurable.

A stands for Achievable

R stands for Realistic.

T stands for Time-bound

Put your long- and short-term goals on paper and stick it on the wall where you spend the most of your time if you want to succeed. If you want to buy an automobile, for example, specify the exact brand, model, year of production, color, and specifications as well as the time and location you would like to make the purchase. If you don't have enough money or can't afford it right now, don't worry about how you're going to pay for it.

WHAT ARE YOUR S.M.A.R.T GOALS?

S= Specific M= Measurable A= Achievable R= Realistic T= Time Bound

1		DATE \ \
2		DATE \ \
3		DATE \ \
4		DATE \ \
5		DATE \ \
6		DATE \ \
7		DATE \ \
8		DATE \ \
9		DATE \ \
10		DATE \ \
11		DATE \ \
12		DATE \ \
13		DATE \ \
14		DATE \ \
15		DATE \ \
16		DATE \ \
17		DATE \ \
18		DATE \ \
19		DATE \ \
20		DATE \ \
21		DATE \ \

I want to talk about my most recent SMART health goals. Upon obtaining my blood test results, I became aware of several health problems. I made a vision board and nailed it to the wall of my study space, including my current and target levels as well as the start and end dates. I also included my diet and exercise plan, and a picture of my role model.

I followed my plan and had my blood tests done again in three months. I was surprised to achieve better than expected results. I was on medication for several years due to a few chronic issues, but those issues have since been resolved. I've cut back on some meds and completely stopped taking others.

My body has also changed to more closely resemble that of my role model. How the universe helps you achieve your SMART goals astounds me. I've been creating vision boards ever since, and I've been successful in accomplishing a lot of my objectives.

Maintaining a journal can be very beneficial in life. I use mine as a productive diary where I assess my seven pillars and write in it every day. I rate each of my pillars from 1 to 5, highlighting my areas of strength and weakness, and work on improving them.

I suggest journaling about the seven pillars for ninety days and seeing how things change.

"You'll never change your life until you change something you do daily. The secret to your success is found in your daily routine."

-- John C. Maxwell

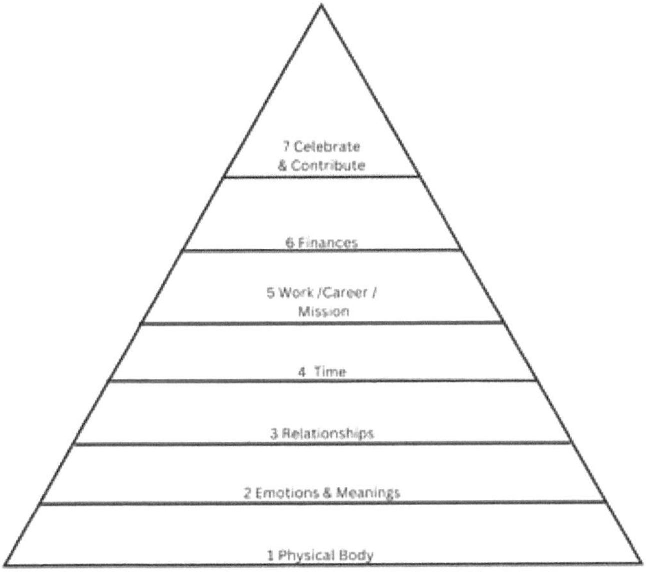

We see lot of people struggle to find fulfillment in their life. Sometimes, even after achieving all the success we forget the fact that in orfer to live a truly fulfilled life, one needs to balance all the pillars of life. These pillars are physicaly body , emotions & meanings, relationship, time, work /career/ mission, finances, and celebration & contribution.

MORNING MINDSET

Date \ \

Affirmation Of The Day

I love money, money loves me. I am a money magnet

Magical Morning

- Affirmations/Visualization ☐
- Prayer/ Gratitude ☐
- Productivity/ Prioritizing ☐
- Learn / Grow / Read ☐
- Exercise / Walk / yoga ☐
- Silence / Meditation ☐

Top 3 Goals / Priorities Of Today

One Or More Person(s)I Would Like To Compliment Today

One Thing I Will Do Out Of My Comfort zone

Today's Schedule

4am-5am

5am-6am

6am-7am

7am-8am

8am-9am

9am-10am

11am-12pm

12pm-1pm

1pm-2pm

2pm-3pm

3pm-4pm

EVENING JOURNAL

Today's Schedule

4pm-5pm

5pm-6pm

6pm-7pm

7pm-8pm

8pm-9pm

9pm-10pm

11pm-12pm

12pm-1pm

1pm-2pm

2pm-3pm

3pm-4pm

My Biggest Achievement Today

What Was My Biggest Learning Today

3 Things I Am Grateful For Today

What Did I Do 1% Better Than Yesterday

What Can I Do Better Tomorrow

Tomorrow's Priorities

About Quantum Life University (QLU)

Brahmarshi Chakravarti Dr. Newton Kondaveti, MBBS, MD, and Brahma Vidvarishta Dr. Lakshmi Newton, MBBS, are physicians who founded Quantum Life University (QLU). Rajashekhar Potluri and Sridevi Potluri served as founding trustees. Shreans Daga, Kiran Anumalasetty, Krishna Mohan Tanguturi, and Sowmya Tanguturi are the other trustee members.

Teachings: Unlocking the Benefits of Spiritual Education.

At QLU, students discover profound truths that go beyond the ordinary while learning from knowledgeable teachers about life's mysteries. By studying sacred teachings on self-awareness, compassion, and wisdom, they discover their own potential and strengthen their bonds with the cosmos. Equipped with this understanding, they meet life's obstacles head-on, exhibiting resilience, peace, and service. "The Eternal Classroom" demonstrates how enlightenment and spiritual education can enhance lives.

I have participated in a number of on-campus and virtual programs. Several of my favorite courses that I have taken or intend to take are as follows:

Doctors Newton Kondaveti, MBBS, MD, and Lakshmi, MD, have taught meditation to millions of people throughout their travels to more than 120 countries.

SOUL COACH TRANSFORMATION PROGRAM (SCTP)

All of the Spiritual Science courses taught at QLU are built upon the foundation provided by the Soul Coach Transformation Program. The Soul Coach Transformation Program seeks to bring your spiritual life on the inside and outside in harmony. It's a system that assists in decluttering your mind, body, and spirit so you can hear the messages from within. It also aids in the discovery of your purpose, enabling you to plan a life that advances that goal.

The majority of participants in the Soul Coach Transformation program see significant and long-lasting changes in their lives. You already possess all the necessary answers. To connect with this wisdom, all you need to do is clear out both your inner and outer clutter. This is a very effective method of getting rid of obstacles that stand in the way of realizing who you truly are. Quantum Life is offering a residential training program that is completely free of charge.

Vikarabad University. The certificate program lasts for ten days. Spiritual Science teaches over 100 topics along with practical tools to help with their application and benefit in day-to-day living. It is held in English, Hindi, and Telugu separately. This program has been attended by thousands of people.

KEY BENEFITS

* Certain subjects will have an immediate, profound impact and influence based on your level of commitment and involvement. As you work on yourself with the guidance given, you will be able to feel the change and transformation that occurs deep within.
* Through all of the social noise and moral conditioning, your true self is revealed.
* One obtains Atma Jnana (Soul Wisdom) by attending all of these classes. Through practice and application of these teachings, one lives from the level of the Soul and ultimately becomes a Brahma Jnani (one who has gained Universal Wisdom).

PAST LIFE REGRESSION

Your entire 'past', encompassing not only your past from this lifetime but also all of your past lifetimes, makes up who you are today. Your subconscious mind stores all of your past experiences and memories, forming the foundation of your personality. By addressing the underlying causes, past-life regression helps to clarify the effects by applying the law of cause and effect. By addressing the underlying cause and figuring out how it has impacted the current situation, significant natural

Healing happens on its own. This principle states that an effect disappears when it is forced back to the cause. Regression to past lives affects the body, mind, emotions, and spirit all at once. It is a holistic healer.

KEY BENEFITS

The comprehension of karmic patterns and the application of this understanding to the treatment of chronic diseases

* Elimination of energy obstacles.

* Finding relief from a wide range of phobias and fears.

* A boost to communication between people.

* The absence of fear of dying.

INNER CHILD WORK

"INNER CHILD WORK" unlocks the Door to the Inner Paradise and provides a comprehensive understanding and healing of the Child Within. The aspect of ourselves that is ultimately alive is referred to as our Inner-Child. The emotional self is the Inner-Child. It is the home of our emotions. Everybody experiences life events that turn into unresolved emotional traumas. Chronic anxiety, fear, confusion, and a sense of emptiness can be caused and exacerbated by the slow accumulation of unresolved mental and emotional issues and misery for the duration of our lives.

KEY BENEFITS

* Start by recognizing and resolving the negative issues that led to your disconnection from your inner child.
* Establish a new connection and integration with your inner child.
* Acquire knowledge on how to nurture and preserve your relationship with your inner child.

BREATH MASTERY

The breath is holy. It has a great deal of power. It carries the life force, which provides us with the essential energy we need to survive. It is the wire that connects us to the boundless reservoir of cosmic energy that underlies all of creation. Breath animates our body, gives our words, chants, and songs energy and force, and helps us cleanse our cells and ourselves. It is the linguistic mother. It can store power or release it into the world, and it can carry immense wisdom—or foolishness. You are a living, breathing light on earth, and that is your universal identity. While you are still in your physical body, this journey with your Sacred Breath will help you realize who you really are.

KEY BENEFITS

* It assists you in releasing the energy blockages influencing your mental, emotional, and physical health.
* It supports your pursuit of spiritual development and inner transformation.
* It aids in your comprehension of the science and art of breathing.

LIFE BETWEEN LIVES (LBL)

The condition in which your soul is between two lives is called "life between lives" (also referred to as "life between life" or "LBL"). It is the time between your spirit departing from your body in the previous life and shortly before you take on a physical form in this one. For everyone seeking spiritual transformation and growth, this is an intense workshop on soul-journey and self-discovery.

KEY BENEFITS

* It helps you discover your Soul Plan and life purpose.
* It supports you in your efforts to grow and transform

spiritually.

* If you are currently involved in holistic or alternative therapy, this training will assist you in incorporating Life Between Lives Regression into your current therapeutic practice.

FAMILY CONSTELLATION

In order to live healthier, happier, and more fulfilled lives, we can break the patterns of stress and trauma that arise in one generation and are passed on to its offspring through a group process. A new direction in life can be chosen in an instant of realization. Transgenerational healing, brought about by family constellation work, enables us to recognize and remove many of the typical roadblocks to our spiritual and personal development.

KEY BENEFITS

* Approach death and serious illness with optimism.
* Recognize the "bigger picture" in every circumstance.
* Clear the air in family relationship misunderstandings, entanglements, and roadblocks.
* End recurring patterns of betrayal, disconnection, abandonment, alienation, abuse, accidents, loss, poverty, etc.
* Break repetitive patterns of abandonment, alienation, abuse, accidents, betrayal, disconnection, dysfunction, loss, poverty, etc.

There are several other programs and workshops which I recommend to visit QLU website www. qluglobal.org or contact QLU staff.

About the author

- I graduated in Project Management from Victoria University, Melbourne.
- I am the founder of AJ Life Mastery, a Learning Management System (LMS) portal.
- I am a Life and Health coach, as well as an Access Bars therapist.
- I am a past life regression therapist.
- I am an author who wrote eBooks on various topics, including chakra mastery.
- I am a founding member of the Australian Multicultural Association Incorporation (AMA) and the Australia Telangana Association Incorporation (ATAI).
- Nominated for Melton Citizen of the Year in 2018.
- Recognised as the best volunteer in 2020 and 2024 for promoting Indian culture and festivals in Australia.
- I served as an advisory board member for Melton Culturally and Linguistically Diverse in the Melton City Council, Victoria, Australia, from 2016 to 2018.
- I have 20 years of experience as an IT consultant.
- I organise women empowerment programs, community radio programs, international student services, Indian arts academies, and other cultural events.
- I am a qualified construction builder and licensed Real Estate agent.

- With 30 years of event organising experience, I have conducted over 300 events during this period.

Valuable insights that aid in navigating day-to-day life.

- I provide business mentoring to individuals, groups, and organisations, assisting with startups, operations, marketing, branding, fundraising, cash flow, business planning, and more. I conduct seminars, workshops, one-to-one sessions, and online sessions.
- I offer teachings in IT (software testing), financial literacy programs, health coaching, and spiritual guidance to resolve personal issues and enhance one's life through aura reading, chakra balancing, and other practices.
- I ran for local councillor elections in the Melton City Council area to serve the residents.
- I have a passion for arts and have produced and directed a short film, as well as promoted arts.

AJ Life Mastery **Dream Girl**

Ajay AV

Ama AV

Testimonials

Amrutha - India

"I am Amruta, and I am very happy to have received a fabulous opportunity to learn and attend Ajay's Chakra balancing course. Before attending Ajay's course, my knowledge of chakras was very limited, and I did not understand how balanced chakras could help achieve a joyful state and fulfil one's life. Ajay's course on Chakra Balancing not only provides knowledge about chakras but also offers steps on how one can balance their chakras in their day-to-day lives using food, Asana Yoga, Beeja Akshari mantra chanting, activities, aromas, crystals, and meditation through visualisation. From the course, I understood that the way we conduct ourselves every moment will align our chakras accordingly. What excited me the most were the food suggestions, activities, and asanas which will help reduce blocks and put us on track towards a joyful state. I would recommend this course to anyone who is inquisitive to learn about chakras and who is ready to implement the homework given by Ajay. I wish all the best to Ajay and happy learning to all future students of Ajay. Thank you so much!"

Sandhya Mantha – Australia

Email ID: sandhya.mantha@yahoo.com

"I was first introduced to Chakras in 2016 by Ajay during a time of profound trauma in my life. Ajay's expertise in assessing and healing my chakras not only alleviated my immediate distress but set me on an entirely new trajectory. Since that pivotal moment, my journey has been nothing short of transformative. Delving into the depths of spirituality, I've unearthed facets of myself I never knew existed, and with each revelation, I've grown immeasurably. Today, I proudly stand as a beacon of healing in multiple disciplines, with Reiki being just one facet of the myriad modalities I now practice. Ajay's guidance was the catalyst for this incredible metamorphosis, and I am forever grateful for his wisdom and support."

Neelima Yeddla – India

Email ID: pavithranaidu0777@gmail.com

"Ajay has been more than just a brother to me; he's been my steadfast support system since our childhood days. His guidance has not only empowered me but also influenced the career choices of my daughters. Despite not being inclined towards meditation or religious rituals, I found myself grappling with severe health issues, financial setbacks, and strained relationships, leaving me devoid of mental peace.

Upon Ajay's suggestion, I reluctantly embarked on a journey of chanting mantras, and to my astonishment, witnessed a profound transformation unfold before me. Miraculously, the pieces of my life began to fall into place. I discovered a dedicated health coach whose guidance led to tangible improvements in my well-being, earning praise from my doctors. Moreover, my children gained clarity in their career paths, and our financial situation took a turn for the better.

With renewed vigour, I renovated our old house into a modern sanctuary, symbolising the positive changes permeating every aspect of our lives. Financial abundance flowed in unprecedented ways, granting me a level of mental peace I had long yearned for. I wholeheartedly believe in Ajay's mission to uplift and transform lives, and I offer him my sincerest wishes for continued success on this noble journey."

Sameen Iqbal Ghosh – Australia

Email ID: Sameen_i@hotmail.com

"Since 2017, I've known Ajay from our collaboration on an event he organised. His guidance transformed my life. Through my community radio program, he advised me on monetisation strategies. Despite being from the Muslim community, Ajay introduced me to meditation and provided mentorship in business, career, and financial growth. His chakra balancing sessions were incredible. Now, I enjoy multiple streams of income, my dream home and car, numerous awards, and immense happiness and respect within my community. I believe the Universe has blessed me through Ajay's teachings. I wholeheartedly support his mission to transform lives and wish him continued success. God bless Ajay."

Uma Shankar – India

Email ID: Shansmartuma@gmail.com

"I'm a civil engineer, and I've been meditating since I was young. Recently, I joined Ajay's online chakra balancing workshop, and it made a big difference in my life. Before, I used to be shy and kept to myself, but Ajay's teachings helped me open up and connect better with others. His guided meditations and unique activities were easy to follow and fit into my daily routine. I wish Ajay the best in his mission to help people change their lives. I highly recommend his book, 'Chakras

Human Manual,' for every household. It's a helpful

guide for dealing with health issues, financial problems, finding peace of mind, and improving relationships. It's like a manual for living and handling everyday challenges. Good luck, Ajay!"

Meera Bommirasipet – India

Email ID: bomi.sachin@gmail.com

"I am a retired school teacher and a spiritual master. A few months ago, I met Ajay, who is my son's friend in Australia. During a long car ride, we engaged in spiritual conversations. Something had been bothering me for a while. Despite attending many satsangs, visiting ashrams, and listening to various spiritual masters, I couldn't find answers to my problems for years. Ajay offered simple solutions that changed my perspective. Now, I lead a peaceful life and maintain good relationships with my loved ones. Ajay has provided clarity on many spiritual questions. I offer my blessings to Ajay on his spiritual journey. With the Grace of God, so be it!"

Kondeti Prakasa Rao – India

Email ID: prakasaraokondeti@gnail.com

"I am a retired botany professor (M. Sc M. Phil). I am a volunteer in Quantum Life University (QLU) campus during SCTP in December 2023 and Inner Child Program in April 2024. Ajay's book on "Chakras Mastery" is a practical guide for all the spiritual seekers. This book is helpful for both physical health and spiritual growth. Ajay was well trained by Dr Newton Kondaveti and Dr Lakshmi Garu at QLU. I was also benefited by his chakra healing. All my blessings and good wishes to Ajay for his mission to transform the lives of the people around the world."

Recommended books

Judith, Anodea. Chakras wheels of life. Mumbai: Jaico Publishing house, 2023. How to use chakras for better health, greater personal power, and expanded spiritual awareness.

Kondaveti, Newton, MD, Consciousness Heals. Hyderabad: Life Publications, 2012. It gives insights of and practical tools to unlock blocked energies.

Kondaveti, Newton, MD, and Lakshmi G.V. MD, Past Life Regression, Hyderabad: Life Publications, 2012. How to eliminate recurring unconscious patterns and gain clarity in personal growth.

Desai, Sneh. Change your Life. Ahmedabad. Sneh World Publication, 2019. Gives practical approach to life, goal setting, resolve issues on day-to-day life.

Castle, Tim. Be the Lion. I_AM self publicating, 2019. Base on 4Cs framework actions on mind, body, self-belief, connections and spirituality. It helps in overcoming big challenges in life.

Committed to the Community
VOTE 1
Ajay
Pasupulate
FOR CAMBRIDGE WARD
MELTON CITY COUNCIL
Authorised by: Geetanjali Muralider - 8 Chancery Way, Taylors Hill VIC 3037

Certificate of Nomination

Ajay Pasupulate

Nominated for 2019 Citizen of the Year
for outstanding contribution to the City of Melton community

Signed

Cr Bob Turner
Mayor
City of Melton

CITY OF MELTON

BEST VOLUNTEER ORGANISATION

AMA

Australian Multicultural Association

Message from :

Sarah Henderson

- Liberal Senator for Victoria.

AMA has been recognised as the best volunteer organisation one among 129 organisations at Federal level for the year 2020.

I write to congratulate your organisation on receiving a grant under the Morrison Liberal Government's Volunteer Grants Program from Gorton.

Your association does such a wonderful job in providing cultural activities and inspiring artistic expression in the Indian community.

www.amainc.org.au

Australian Multicultural Association

www.amainc.org.au amainc@gmail.com